Seeds for the FUTURE

Lake Hickory Resources

James H. Royston, Executive Editor
George W. Bullard Jr., Senior Editor

**Spiritual Leadership in a Secular Age: Building Bridges
Instead of Barriers**
Edward H. Hammett

**Operation Inasmuch: Mobilizing Believers beyond
the Walls of the Church**
David W. Crocker

**Seeds for the Future: Growing Organic Leaders
for Living Churches**
Robert D. Dale

Pursuing the Full Kingdom Potential of Your Congregation
George W. Bullard Jr.

Available at
www.lakehickoryresources.com

Seeds for the FUTURE

Growing Organic Leaders for Living Churches

ROBERT D. DALE

Lake Hickory RESOURCES
ST. LOUIS, MISSOURI

Cover art: FotoSearch
Cover and interior design: Elizabeth Wright

See more Lake Hickory resources at
www.lakehickoryresources.com.

10 9 8 7 6 5 4 3 2 1   05 06 07 08 09 10

Library of Congress Cataloging-in-Publication Data

Dale, Robert D.
  Seeds for the future : growing organic leaders for living churches / Robert D. Dale.
    p. cm.
  Includes bibliographical references.
  ISBN-10: 0-827234-64-3
  ISBN-13: 978-0-827234-64-2
  (pbk. : alk. paper)
  1. Christian leadership. I. Title.
BV652.1.D345 2005
253–dc22

                                              2005016077

Printed in the United States of America

To Larry Matthews,

friend, mentor,

and fellow explorer of systemic leadership.

Contents

Inspiration and Wisdom for Twenty-first–Century Christian Leaders

You have chosen wisely in deciding to study and learn from a **Lake Hickory Resources** book. Lake Hickory Resources publishes for

- congregational leaders who desire to serve effectively
- Christian ministers who pursue excellence in service
- members of a congregation that desires to reach its full Kingdom potential
- denominational leaders who want to come alongside affiliated congregations in a servant leadership role

Lake Hickory Resources is an inspiration- and wisdom-sharing vehicle of Lake Hickory Learning Communities. LHLC is the web of relationships developing from the base of Hollifield Leadership Center (www.Hollifeld.org) near Hickory, North Carolina. LHLC addresses emerging strategic issues of leadership development for congregations, denominations, and parachurch organizations.

The mission of **Lake Hickory Resources** currently is being expressed through two meaningful avenues. First, George Bullard, executive coach for Lake Hickory Learning Communities, also is senior editor for *Net Results* magazine (www.NetResults.org), a national, transdenominational publication that appears monthly in print and electronic form.

Second, **Lake Hickory Resources** publishes books in partnership with Christian Board of Publication. Once this partnership is in full production it will produce eight to twelve new books each year.

We welcome your comments on these books, and we welcome your suggestions for new subject areas and authors we ought to consider.

James H. Royston, Executive Editor
George W. Bullard Jr., Senior Editor
SeniorEditor@LakeHickoryResources.org
Lake Hickory Learning Communities is a ministry of
www.NorthCarolinaBaptists.org

Preface

I was wrong. Dead wrong. And I've repented and tried to start over again.

A few weeks ago a former student of mine from seminary days joined a group for a presentation I was making. "I've come to see if you're still making the same speech as twenty-five years ago," he announced with tongue-in-cheek. The rest of the group laughed at his comment. I answered, "I've repented of my sins." And, the group laughed again.

I made my presentation on how pastors lead, demonstrating how my mind has changed. My former student listened carefully and agreed. My approach to leadership has changed 180 degrees. I have moved from being a CEO-style leader to being a cultivator-oriented leader.

Living Churches, Organic Leaders

However, it was a long time coming. I became a pastor in the last few months of the 1950s, and served local churches into the 1970s, when mechanical thinking completely ruled the Western world. Then, I spent five years traveling the United States conducting pastoral leadership seminars, transitioned to a seminary classroom for a dozen years of teaching young ministers to lead churches, and in 1989 moved to Virginia to direct a leadership center and serve on the leader team for the Virginia Baptist Mission Board. From the beginning, I'd baptized the latest and greatest business models and translated them to religious settings, where they were immediately and always at least a bit ill-fitting and ill-suited to volunteer-led churches.

Along the way, I'd seen the result of treating living communities like machines. I'd watched some leaders crash and burn, create conflict, shrink churches, and sink into despair. But, most crucially, I'd realized that the New Testament didn't assume the same machine-driven mindsets the West has taken for granted for so long. In fact, it finally dawned on me that our American perspective is so ingrained that our secular views have dominated leaders, including those of us who insist we are following strictly biblical principles. We simply don't question–or even identify–our scientific assumptions. When I started framing congregational leadership in living and organic images, people quickly agreed. Then, some of them, similar to the "Rich Young Ruler," went away sadly. They said they couldn't–or wouldn't–change to leadership approaches that didn't match what they'd always thought about leadership–even if organic approaches meshed with the New Testament and matched the hungers of the emerging church. So, the quest began that brings us to *Seeds for the Future*. Let's begin at the most elementary level–a seed.

Potential—Seeds for the Future

A seed is a promise, a potentiality. Several years ago during the Soviet era, an American was traveling through a farming area in Russia while they experienced a terrible famine. People were literally starving. Piles of seed wheat for the next year's crop stood in each of the village squares. The American asked a naïve, short-term question, "Why don't you eat the seed wheat?" The Russian host gave a wiser, longer-term answer, "You never steal from the future." Seeds are our future.

What's more basic than a seed? A seed is a beginning, an embryo, a source, and an origin. Planting or transplanting a seed is an act of faith. A single seed holds potential for new life, then new growth, and finally new harvest. Today's seeds foreshadow tomorrow's flowers, forests, and friends.

Jesus told a great story about a farmer who sowed seeds (Mt. 13:3–9). The parable describes three kinds of inhospitable soil:

1. hard paths where the birds eat the seeds that have no entry point into a seedbed
2. rocky soil where the roots are prevented from growing deep enough to support newly sprouted life
3. crowded seedbeds where new plants are quickly choked out

However, those seeds that landed on receptive soil produced one hundred or sixty or thirty fold.

Sowing good seeds in good soil is a basic planting formula. Whether you're a gardener or a congregational leader, your organic growth challenge always involves sowers, seeds, and seedbeds.

This growing guide emerges from a conviction and a confession. I am convinced that the church of Jesus Christ is alive. I confess that up to now we haven't always led it as a living organism.

So think of the ideas that follow as a seed catalog, a planting and growing guide for leader-gardeners in living churches. Growing "organic" leaders–lively, living leaders for lively, living churches–is the hope and focus of this book.

Reading This Book

Although becoming a leader is a lifelong process, this book is designed for rapid-fire reading. I've used bold headlines to give one-sentence summaries of each chapter; bullets; boxes; visual models; "leader's lexicons" to define new terms; brief case studies; and coaching conversations to sum up and highlight key ideas. Additionally, I've cited lots of ideas in the endnotes for follow-up as your interest grows. Even with these shortcuts, I hope you'll read this book carefully, letting lots of seeds fall into your life and into your practice of leadership.

Let me post a warning at the beginning. On every page that follows, I'll ask you to think about and to practice pastoral leadership in a new way. It is not easy to change our minds and our ministries. I'm proposing that we lead our faith communities in organic fashion.

Organic leaders sow and grow. For four hundred years, leaders have practiced "pry and push" leadership. We've used mechanical approaches drawn from the levers and hydraulics of the Industrial Age. These approaches have created images and the practice of pressurized leadership. The Bible and current thinking styles are guiding us toward sowing seeds of ministry and growing believers toward leadership. "Sow and grow" leaders are the seeds of the future. For organic leaders, sowing and growing is job one. "Sow and grow" is the alpha and omega for organic leaders.

That's new and challenging. Living things have infinite ways of relating to our world and offer many organic images for us to draw on as leaders. As you read, you'll see a wide array of organic images. It's the way God made our world. And, it's the only way I know to help us confront old thinking patterns and launch new ones. Welcome to the emerging field of organic leadership.

Acknowledgments

Books germinate and grow slowly over time. Lots of people have been involved in sowing the seeds for this book. I want to thank a small array of persons–out of many–for the seeds they planted and cultivated in me. Many of these persons became partners and fellow learners in professional and personal growth from projects we conducted through the Center for Creative Church Leadership Development, now the Ray and Ann Spence Network for Congregational Leadership.

My thanks go especially to Larry Matthews, to whom this book is dedicated. Larry has opened systems' practices to me in ever deeper and more meaningful ways as we've worked for many years with two training processes–our Young Leaders' Program and our Leading Church Systems amid Change.

Virginia Tech's Master Gardener Program reawakened and expanded my interest in growing things. That training process had a hand in pointing me back to the basic organic nature of Christ's church in the New Testament and indirectly reshaping my view of leadership.

I'm grateful as well to Brian Williams and Bob Perry, colleagues in leader growth, who continue to stimulate me to grow as a leader through their restless pursuit of the new, the needed, the theological, and the organic.

The Four Horsemen–my reading group made up of Keith Smith, John Chandler, Mike Clingenpeel, and myself–submerges me each month in books that I'd not necessarily choose myself. This intellectual dunking, some of it in hot water and some of it in holy water, shows up throughout this book.

Bert Browning, Gary Chapman, and Cassidy Dale read early drafts and gave helpful and appreciated feedback.

I'm glad my family stretches my horizons every day. Cass keeps my eye focused on futures. Amy sharpens my artistic eye. Carrie, family cheerleader, keeps her eyes open and applauds when I express ideas well.

PART 1

Cultivating Sowers, Seeds, and Seasons

Life moves in triads. Storytellers and teachers have used threes to unfold tales and truth to us for ages. We call this approach the rule of three.

We see this pattern in Scripture. Abraham, Isaac, and Jacob. Father, Son, and Holy Spirit. Prodigal son, waiting father, and unhappy elder son and brother. Faith, hope, and love. Priest, Levite, and good Samaritan on the Jericho Road. Creator, Judge, and Redeemer. Peter, James, and John. "Holy, holy, holy is the Lord God Almighty, who was, and is, and is to come" (Rev. 4:8).[1]

The same device of "triplicity" is common in secular stories, advertising, and world history as well. Tom, Dick, and Harry. The three little pigs, the three blind mice, the Three Stooges. Small, medium, large. Snap, crackle, pop. Green, yellow, red traffic lights. The good, bad, and ugly. "I came, I saw, I conquered," announced Caesar of his Pontic campaign. Beginning, middle, and end.

Leaders have also long recognized that leadership is triadic: leaders, followers, and systems or settings.[2] As leaders,

- we cultivate our selves and souls as lifelong growers
- we live within and lead living communities
- we live and lead in a era of change, a context that's already in progress

Leadership is a conversation that flows in three directions. In fact, congregations blend three stories—the leaders' story, the community's story, and the contextual story.

Leaders understand—or at least intuit—the two elements of triads we can influence. Leaders relate to and communicate with followers in our communities. Leaders minister in settings and contexts. But, we can't force followers and settings or contexts to interact. That's the indirect, "off-side" of the relationship and is beyond our reach.

Taking direct responsibility for indirect relationships within triads is messianic.

In organic fashion, hear and respond to the give-and-take between leaders, communities, and contexts in the first three chapters:

- Growing Self, Growing Soul
- Your Church Is Alive
- Already in Progress

CHAPTER 1

Growing Self, Growing Soul

Remember how much you wanted to grow and "be big" when you were a little kid? Remember standing against a door facing and stretching to your fullest height while Mom or Dad marked your growth and progress? Remember how pleased you were when someone bragged, "You're growing like a weed!"? Today's congregations need big, robust, growing leaders to match our ministry opportunities. Are you ready to grow as a congregational leader?

A Home Improvement Store for Leaders?

Leaders are clear why we're here. Character, integrity, trustworthiness, and belief are some of the basic wellsprings for leaders, but they aren't easily won. Growing ourselves as leaders is a lifelong pilgrimage of personal, professional, and spiritual development. God uses time to teach us life's deeper lessons. After all, as living entities, we are more than static "human beings." We are dynamic "human becomings."

Becoming a leader is a learn-as-you-go process, a do-it-yourself project. Our selves and souls are the raw materials for leadership. Unfortunately, there's no home improvement store or handy garden center for growing leaders. The good news is that as living beings, we have our whole lives to learn to live and lead well. The bad news is it often takes our entire lifespan, constant discipline, and support from our faith community and others to grow our selves and our souls toward leadership. That's not what lots of today's church leaders expect or want to hear. Our world is an in-an-instant, find-a-shortcut, microwave-quick, leader-tricks-for-dummies culture. So taking time to grow depth, breadth, and height is not apt to become number 1 in the hearts and minds of many impatient or pressured leaders. But when we think about leadership organically and theologically, we find no other way to grow ourselves and garden[1] our souls.

LEADER'S LEXICON

"Organic Leadership," the practice of leading by sowing seeds of ministry and growing believers into leaders, or leading by "sow and grow" actions.

Aquifers: Deeper Sources of Self and Soul

Our sense of grounding, flowing from identity and faith, is largely invisible until we act as leaders. Then, behaviors reflecting identity and faith reveal obvious sources of strength or weakness. These foundations are like aquifers.

LEADER'S LEXICON

"Aquifer," a body of rock that collects and conducts water underground, and, in this case, a metaphor of deep resources for growth.

Aquifers, those underground reservoirs or water storage areas providing our water supply, are deep and hidden sources of life. They remain unseen and taken for granted...until they run dry. At that point, the wellsprings, literally the watery resources for wells and springs, evaporate. Although the earth's surface is about 70 percent water, only about 1 percent of that amount is drinkable fresh water. Without those imperceptible aquifers, humans would go thirsty...and even die. That metaphor is telling for leaders. We're called to invest in the deeper, less visible sources of life and leadership or die.

How can we grow as leaders? Is there a formal "curriculum" for growing self and soul for leaders? Or is the development of good leaders just a happy accident? Lots of religious books on leadership are available, mostly inspirational in tone or exegetical in structure. Oddly, while these books are broadly *about* leadership, few have any actual theory of what leaders do or how they do it. They list characteristics of leaders or do biblical studies *about* leadership. Although these materials are interesting and inspiring, they offer very little on developing healthy leaders for religious communities, and even less on the central challenge of growing leaders for God's kingdom. That's a fault of a mechanistic perspective. In the Industrial Age, the debate was about whether leaders were made or born, implying an assembly line for leaders. But, with an organic mindset, the challenge is growing leaders and cultivating a theory of leadership for them to practice.

Actually, many streams flow together in the growth and formation of healthy leaders. Here are the streams we'll navigate on leader growth:

- Family systems
- Models and mentors
- Relationship gifts
- Core beliefs
- Key supporters
- Defining moments
- Early opportunities to practice leadership
- Opportunities to start over
- A theory of congregational leadership

These tributaries and other feeders are basic shapers of life and leaders. Other feeders also flow into those aquifers that make us the unique persons and leaders we are.

Becoming Clear about Why You're Here

As a practitioner's art, leadership is largely a self-taught and soul-grown craft. We learn as we go, if we learn from our failures and successes. Truth be told, we rarely step back from our lives and identify our key sources of self and soul. Let's offer ourselves the gift of perspective. Stated in organic images, plants are more often judged by their foliage than by their root systems. But, it's the root system that gives life to the foliage and fruit. The same is true for leaders. To frame the leader's growth challenge in grammatical terms, leaders need nouns more than adjectives, identifiers more than modifiers. Nouns name us. They tell who we are and what we stand for. Robert Fulghum, the popular author, has one word on his business card: "Fulghum." That's all he needs–one name, one noun, no adjectives. His calling in life is simple: "What I do is to be the most Fulghum I can be."[2] Adjectives limit or qualify basic identity and should only be added to our identities with great caution. Think roots and think nouns as you explore your own growth as a leader.

Clarity about why you're here as a leader may come to you at life's most potent intersections. Frederick Buechner describes that intersection well: "The place you're called to be is the place where your deep gladness and the world's deep need meet."[3] That telling crossroads may loom up on us from an array of mostly inner experiences. Leadership is an inside-out process. This journey inward–journey outward process moves from spirit to practice. Warren Bennis notes that "leaders are people who are able to express themselves fully...[T]hey know who they are, what their strengths and weaknesses are, and they know how to fully deploy their strengths and compensate for their weaknesses."[4]

So let's explore our spiritual and psychological aquifers and "read" the emergence of self and soul in a broad biblical format. I hope you'll squelch the impulse to "speed read" this chapter and give each section some "soak time" to draw from the aquifers in your past, present, and future.

Family Roots: Abraham, Isaac, Jacob, and Our Personal Patriarchs and Matriarchs

The story of leadership in the Bible begins with a family, with stories of the patriarchs and matriarchs. In fact, this Old Testament tale revolves around a family of families, a multigenerational mosaic. In Genesis 12:1–3, God promises Abram three things: land, ancestry, and blessing. Then, as the saga unfolds across decades and generations, the plot thickens to reveal that this particular family system would make God's promises difficult to fulfill.

LEADER'S LEXICON

"Family Systems," a view of human interaction that assumes our behavior patterns are shaped by our families of origin and transmitted across generations.

Abram's family and lineage were nomads, making a land of their own a distant dream. They tended to be infertile, causing the prospect of children as numerous as sand on the seashores to seem pretty farfetched. They were selfish and deceptive, creating long odds that they would become a redemptive minority blessing the majority of the world. Some readers must wonder if God can grow his promises to maturity from such imperfect seeds. But, thank God, leaders don't have to be perfect or to come from perfect families to serve well.

Some leadership experts feel leadership is more caught than taught, especially early in life. Have you heard the provocative idea that the role you filled in your family of origin is the role you'll adopt in future organizational settings where you lead and follow?[5] The concept is that family roles are so indelibly engraved in our lives that the patterns are deeply rooted.[6] The bottom line is that faces change from generation to generation, but functions are passed along and endure across time.

If organizations are somehow surrogate families and if congregations are somehow second-chance families, form is apt to follow function. Emotional process wins just about every day, since our genes and memes are such strong shapers of behavior.[7]

How did you function in your family of origin? What role did you fill? There are far too many options for an exhaustive list, but some common possibilities are noted below.

- The Heir Apparents, usually blessed firstborn sons or daughters who serve as family flag-bearers, lending the promise of a future, generally overfunctioning by taking on heavy responsibilities, and carrying family or organizational traditions forward

- The Challengers, like Isaac, the children who destroy the parents' idols, become rivals, and eventually replace the parents and organizational leaders

- Favored Children, like Joseph, placing them in competition with other members of the family or organization

- The Rebels—the prodigal sons or daughters—who face rejection by adopting roles of the maverick who forges independent directions or the risk taker who combines courage and creativity in family circles and work life[8]

- The Queen-Makers or King-Makers, like Mordecai to Esther, who give the younger generations some settings and situations in which they can emerge into new roles

- The Mentors, like Barnabas to Paul or Paul to Timothy and John Mark, who believe in, bless, and coach emerging leaders so the younger leaders can finally fly solo and take the helm

- The Mothers or Fathers, whose jobs are to grow people as they lead families and organizations

- The Brothers and Sisters, who—although not necessarily related by kin ties—treat each other like family and, as equals, help each other navigate the legacies, challenges, and disappointments of home as well as board rooms

- The Sibling Rivals, who not only compete but who may undercut and scapegoat one another
- The Spoiled Brats, who are willing to be obnoxious to gain what they want from situations

Have you seen these kinsmen and fellow workers? Which of these roles have you seen yourself filling? Remember that some family examples will be positive, and others are apt to be negative; but all are powerful shapers of future behavior. Doing your own family diagram or genogram to discover themes and triangles is a powerful developmental process for leaders.[9]

Think about the leadership lessons you learned from the family that shaped you. Ask yourself the following questions about leadership issues to see what behaviors you may have "caught" from your family.

- Who showed you how to make decisions?
- Who showed you how to take initiative?
- Who showed you how to take risks?
- Who "cradled" you in basic theology?

COACHING CONVERSATION

One challenge of leaders is to identify and really understand the implications of how we functioned in our families of origin. Then, armed with more insight and foresight, we may be able to be intentional rather than habitual in the ways we relate to our leadership communities. Most of our family heritage, especially the patterns related to leadership, flies under our emotional radar and gets repeated without notice or evaluation. Family archetypes are among life's deepest and least tapped aquifers. To gain new perspectives on who we are and how we lead, leadership coaches and other wise counselors may become our vital allies along the growth journey.

Hybrid Heroes and Heroines: Major and Minor Prophets in Our Lives

"You make me want to be a better man," said the Jack Nicholson character in the movie, *As Good As It Gets.* Who are the people in your life who have and do make you aspire to be a better person and a better leader? Those folks are your heroes and heroines, your models and mentors. Or, stated another way, they are your "major prophets."

Mentors are special people in our lives. In Greek mythology, Mentor was friend and advisor to Odysseus and guardian to Odysseus's son. Our mentors likewise help us grow in the direction of our goals. Typically, our mentors are a generation or so older and are already experienced in the world we're approaching. Adopting us on the basis of special relational chemistry, they choose us, guide us, sponsor us, teach us, and make us their apprentices.

The mentor-apprentice relationship is intense and unique. Part friend, part parent, but fully neither, mentors nurture our calling. Mentoring relationships usually last from two to ten years. They may, like the ministry partnership between Paul and Barnabas, end painfully when they "had such a sharp disagreement that they parted company" (Acts 15:39). In the meantime, mentors help us find and follow our passion. One clue in the Paul and Barnabas story is the mentoring watershed: We need mentors the first half of our life as we look for success, and we become mentors during the second half of life as we search for significance.[10]

In my own life, Claude McFerron made me want to be a better person. "Mac" was my pastor–twice–during my early years. My family moved from one area to another, from one church to another. Mac first served the Cave Springs church and then the Sweetwater church. Mac became my pastoral model. His heart made an impression on me. He was someone who literally loved people into the kingdom of God. I heard him preach many sermons, but I only remember the words and theme of one.[11] I spent time with him at church and in members' homes, but I don't recall him trying deliberately to teach me to be a leader. I just remember that he cared about me, invested time in me, and believed in my potential. Mac baptized me and helped me choose a college where I could pursue my calling. Along the way, I learned how to connect to a community of faith, how to relate to all kinds of people, how to grow into a person of faith, and how to lead–all without any "overt lessons." His example was contagious, and I caught it.

Twenty years into ministry I was leading a seminar in one of the airport hotels in Kansas City, and, to my surprise, Claude McFerron walked into the ballroom. When I greeted him and asked what brought him all the way from Waterloo, Iowa, for a two-hour presentation, he said, "You." I was floored. But, that was Mac. He loved the communities he led, and he cared about the people who were in those congregations. Mac was and remains my mentor and hero in ministry. He made me want to be a better person, a better Christian, and a better congregational leader. He's still my "major prophet," my model of pastoral leadership.

An acid test of mentoring parallels Charles M. Sheldon's classic 1896 novel, *In His Steps*, with its basic question: "What would Jesus do?"[12] You know you have a mentor when you ask, "What would my mentor do?" Like Claude McFerron in my own case, mentors show the way and make you want to be a better person and leader. Whose name goes in that "What would ____ do" question? That person has a developmental relationship with you and is a mentor for you.

We usually know our mentors "up close and personal." We've seen and admired their work firsthand. But our models may be more distant from us in time and type. Models can be historical figures we've studied, program personalities we enjoy, authors we appreciate, or media types we see. Mentors and models have a common, critical impact on us—we want to "be like" them. They are our "major prophets."

Our "minor prophets," on the other hand, are likely those friends or strategic bystanders who just happened to be with us when we arrived at some of life's pivotal crossroads. They shared a turning point with us and gave us moral support. I've only had four or five of these special people in my entire life.

George Kalemkarian, my Sunday school teacher in the Sweetwater church while I was in high school, was an unlikely minor prophet for me. In the first place, George was not similar to anyone else in our rural church in our insular Ozark Mountain community. He was educated, an electrical engineer. He was an Armenian from California and a preacher's kid. And, he was only in our church for a few years. However, he was in my life at a ripe moment and helped me to cross a key intersection in my life. When I was wrestling with my sense of calling into ministry during college, I went to George's home to ask his advice. He listened and affirmed me. I can't recall what he said, but somehow he blessed me. That was all I needed. I don't recall ever talking with George again. But, he had been in the right place at the right time to help me move in the right direction. I'm grateful for George and a very few others who have been my minor prophets at major crossroads.

- Can you identify major and minor prophets in your life?
- How did you choose each other?
- Which of their gifts or strengths have you imitated?
- How have they clarified your values and helped you take the high road?
- Have you thanked them for serving as emotional and spiritual aquifers, as sources of depth, breadth, and height for you?

Living and Leading Well: Wisdom Writings and People Smarts

Trying to live a godly life is a baseline goal for religious leaders. The Bible is full of wisdom writings, materials that orient our lives toward God and help us choose well as we relate to people. Mostly found in the Old Testament, especially Proverbs, Job, Ecclesiastes, the Song of Solomon, and some psalms, these teachings are practical and values-based. Much of the wisdom literature focuses on healthy human relationships.

Being wise involves more than just having a high IQ. Recent research has discovered much about being "people smart," or about demonstrating "EQ," or emotional intelligence.[13] The vast majority of our personal and professional success results from our ability to understand ourselves and to deal with others well. Personally and internally, how self-aware we are and how well we manage ourselves is foundational. Interpersonally and externally, how socially attuned we are and how we handle relationships is critical. In other words, our ease in relationships revolves around how accurately we read ourselves, how well we regulate ourselves, and how fully we use our social radar as we deal with others.

Soul Gardening: Carpentry Shops, Calling, and Our Faith Communities

Jesus' early life was steeped in the religious practices of his tradition and its laws. His parents took him to the temple when he was eight days old, where he was named and circumcised (Lk. 2:21). Jesus went to Jerusalem at age twelve and astonished religious leaders with his questions and understanding. He demonstrated that he was growing physically, intellectually, spiritually, and relationally (Lk. 2:40, 52). It's no stretch to assume that Jesus and his family worshiped and studied regularly at their home synagogue.

Until he was thirty, Jesus worked in the family business, the carpentry shop in Nazareth. As a craftsman, he perhaps developed a strategic sense that would later serve him well as a leader. Remember that carpenters of that era designed their own projects, cut and cured their own wood, and shaped the requested item from scratch. That ability to see the big picture, envision a specific outcome, focus on what had to be done, and see a project to completion is basic for strategic leadership.[14] Then, at thirty, he answered his calling, was baptized, and launched his redemptive ministry (Lk. 3:21–23). It's significant to note that Jesus invested nearly a year in private soul gardening for every month he spent in public ministry.

LEADER'S LEXICON

"Soul Gardening," a spiritual discipline of cultivating inner depth and breadth.

Investing time and effort in the aquifers of the spirit is always energy well spent for religious leaders. Soul gardening for most of us requires attention to the seasons of our spirits. It's a balancing act to develop a renewal routine and still blend variety and new elements into the pattern. Obviously, there's no one-size-fits-all solution. The challenge is to discern God at work in our lives. What fits the rhythms of routine-variety for you as a leader? Here are a few possibilities for your consideration.

- Steeping ourselves in sacred writings is basic and traditional. A pastor friend reads and meditates on a psalm and a hymn each day. I love the story of the prodigal son, so *The Return of the Prodigal Son* by Henri Nouwen is a personal devotional favorite.[15]

- Experiencing the power of God's Spirit expands our horizons and ignites us to make a difference in our congregations and our world.[16] These experiences typically are community-based and give us a foretaste of leadership.

- Variety in spiritual formation can be designed into your practices deliberately. One spiritual director asks his students to choose one biblical writer, one theological writer, and one spiritual discipline—and then to focus on those resources for an entire year. The next year, then, brings a new rotation.[17]

- Daily practice of prayer is a bedrock discipline for most of us. One friend of mine prays each morning for everyone who works on his floor of his office building. That practice structured some of his prayers and sensitized him to the work community with whom he spent large chunks of his days.

- Seasons of the church year provide themes for us to explore to deepen our spiritual lives as leaders.[18] The rhythms of our souls are reflected in life's seasons.

- Prayer "triggers" offer another option. An acquaintance pauses to intercede every time she hears a siren. Her assumption is that someone is in crisis and needs all of the strength and solace that can be mustered.[19]

- Belonging to faith communities is a common way to keep your spiritual roots reaching deeper and deeper into meaning and memories. We're part of an ongoing family of faith. When we sit in the shade, we can be sure someone else planted the tree long ago as an act of faith. News stories and movies may also trigger our prayers.

- Novels about matters of faith and ministry or personal accounts give us another way to compare our spiritual journeys to others' pilgrimages.[20]

COACHING CONVERSATION

The central issue is not so much what you read, where you belong, or even what you do to grow self and soul. It's that you take deliberate steps to grow as a person and a leader, especially if you need to do some remedial work to mend "holes in your soul."[21]

Support Networks: Inner Circles and Our Special Friends

Jesus had an inner circle—Peter, James, and John—who shadowed him throughout his ministry. They were companions, learners, and, on occasion, encouragers. In other situations, they didn't "get it" and showed Jesus that leadership can be a lonely calling.

Although they aren't infallible themselves, the chosen persons in *our* inner circles see us at our stellar best *and* our fallible worst. They tell us the truth, use trust as a stimulant in our development, lend perspective through intensive feedback, steady us by dampening our anxiety down, trim our egos, and, in spite of all our foibles, may still give us the benefit of the doubt. They keep us from believing our own spines are the actual axes of the universe.[22] They open our eyes to larger sight lines, fresher options, and calmer decisions. They stretch our viewpoints beyond our narrow backgrounds and experiences. Like the "clearness committees" in Quaker tradition, our supporters hold our feet to the fire and help us discern the workings of God in our lives.[23]

This special category of relationship—spouse, best friend, parent, confessor, therapist, work partner, physician, and spiritual director—forms an exclusive group. These associates in our "inner circle" are few and far between. They are the select, core members of our support networks for life and leadership. Precisely because they are rare, they are precious resources to help us drill deep into leadership's aquifers.

Would you be willing to assess your support network? Begin with a clean sheet of paper. List all the persons whom you consider to be part of your personal and professional inner circle. Now let's evaluate the list for breadth, balance, and rigor:

- Strike the names of all of your family members from the list. Don't misunderstand. Family members are typically among our best encouragers. But, they may not be our most objective guides.

- From the remaining names, strike off persons who live more than one hundred miles away from you and persons with whom you don't have direct contact at least every six weeks. Even in these days of e-mail and cell phones, ongoing face-to-face conversations are preferred with your inner circle. Easy accessibility, leisurely pace, and the ability to read nonverbal signals are vital to quality support.

- If some names still remain on your list, strike off persons who share your same vocation or are a part of your denominational family. Too often religious leaders fall into the "birds of a feather flock together" school of leader support, making our inner circle a setting for shop talk only, rather than dealing with larger and deeper issues of leader development.

COACHING CONVERSATION

Return to the wellsprings of the aquifer metaphor. Your support network offers depth, objectivity, and refreshment for you. How do you rate the strength of your encouragers in life and leadership?

White Hot Crucibles: Temptations, Gethsemane, and Our Crises

When Jesus stepped onto the public stage of ministry, he was immediately confronted by temptations, the lure of bad short cuts to good goals. Then, later in his ministry as he approached his death on the cross, he endured Gethsemane—a heart-searching, soul-crushing experience for Jesus. Like bookends, these two crucibles of the temptations and Gethsemane framed Jesus' ministry. And, like crucibles are apt to do, these focusing experiences shaped his decisions and directions.

Crucibles, from the Latin for "cross," mold us. These severe trials of faith and character are lessons we learn by heart. They either make us better and stronger, or they crush us. It's no accident that in science, a crucible refers to a container that resists great heat. Crucibles—wars[24], economic depressions, family crises, health traumas, faith challenges—are defining moments for self and soul.[25] They give meaning to life's pivot points, create memories from touchstone experiences, and stir deep, aquifer-quality questions.

- Who am I?
- Who will I become?
- How will the inner me relate to the outer "crosses" of my world?

When I examine the several crucibles in my life, my brother's bone marrow transplant ranks as the most critical for my learning. He was diagnosed with leukemia and told his only chance for life and health lay in a transplant. After testing, I was identified as his best match and became his donor. In 1992 the transplant process was brutal. The patient's immune system was methodically destroyed with massive doses of radiation. When the point of death was reached, a rescue was attempted with the infusion of a new bone marrow. Then, the longer-term battle became fighting off rejection of the graft and protecting the fledgling immune system.

Several personal defining discoveries grew out of the crucible of the transplant process for me.

Sometimes Crisis Chooses You

Neither my brother nor I welcomed anything about the prospect of his transplant. If we had been given options, we would have chosen to be somewhere else doing almost anything else. I suppose we could have felt victimized and angry. But we were more philosophical about the entire process. As the joke goes, "Sometimes you're the windshield, and sometimes you're the bug." Sometimes the crucible of crisis and hardship chooses you. Then, you can make the unintentional into an intentional growth experience. You try to cope. You try to learn. You try to survive. You try to go on. And, you do.

You Can Survive More Than You Think

Transplant hospitals are highly regimented settings. Your life and schedule aren't your own. You're told where to go, when to show up, and what to do. But, that's part of dealing with this kind of crisis. Structure helps you survive. Shifting to autopilot lets you lean on the frameworks of the day and step into the unknown.

The sheer task of moment-to-moment survival can get pretty dramatic. You see three-year-olds who have never known health. The patient in the room next to my brother was undergoing his third transplant, a struggle beyond imagination. The nurse-to-patient ratio was only 1:4, and their skill was matched by the intensity of the fight for life happening in every hospital room. Our chaplain, Percy Randle, a transplant survivor himself, was a guide, comforter, and friend. Taken an hour at a time, you can make it. Living things have a greater capacity for surviving than we often think.

It Does "Take a Village" to Survive and Thrive

The staff members at our transplant hospital were amazing. Volunteers met us at the airport and helped us settle into our apartment. The intake doctors were kind, patient, but very frank in describing our situation and its options. Social workers provided family support groups. Pain doctors, nutritionists, and researchers offered expertise and encouragement. And, of course, friends and family members called, sent cards, offered money, and prayed for miracles. When you've "walked the plank" and are standing over the abyss, you realize how none of us survives alone. Surviving and thriving takes an entire village of persons who care about us.

My brother came through his successful transplant process with the normal crises and setbacks. Within a few months he was back home in Colorado and planning a return to work. Then tragedy struck. An abscessed tooth—without the protection and resilience of a strong immune system—killed him. His death created another village of support and concern for those of us who gathered to celebrate his life and live in his absence.

Crisis—and our response to it—is a make-or-break occasion. Community support keeps those crushing experiences of life from literally crushing the life out of us. After a crucible has squeezed us, it's important to pause and harvest lessons—personal and professional—for the future.

First Harvest: Antioch and Missionary Journeys, Places for Us to Learn (and to Fail Safely)

Pentecost unleashed the faithful followers of Christ. As threats of persecution scattered believers, they planted churches everywhere. Beginning with the Jews and then reaching out to the Gentiles, the gospel took root and grew rapidly. One of the first gardens of faith sprang up at Antioch. Paul's one-year internship in ministry happened there with Barnabas as his mentor (Acts 11:22–26). We assume Antioch was a good seminary for Paul. From that point, Paul and Barnabas launched their missionary journeys together and separately.

Early experiences in leadership and first jobs in ministry have a make-or-break quality about them. They shape who we are and how we relate. They mold our sense of confidence about ourselves as leaders. First-time leadership experiences stretch our horizons, test our attitudes and skills, and push us beyond our comfort zones.

I've led Young Leaders' Programs for nearly twenty years. I always ask when these high-potential young leaders first realized that others saw them as leaders. Most were given leadership responsibilities as pre-teens or teenagers. Most of them emerged as leaders at school in music, government, or sports, and at church in their youth groups. In these settings, they received responsibility to test their wings. Here also they found refuge in case they crashed. Our early practice of leadership is formative. We all need persons who help us hone the crafts of leadership, places to learn, and places to fail safely.

Failure is a powerful teacher for most of us, making the safety of failing with people who nurture us a godsend. In our Young Leaders' Program, I also inquire about these fledgling ministers' most obvious successes and failures. They report learning from their breakthrough successes, but their more profound lessons grow out of their failures. When they report what failure has taught them, I'm always impressed by how quickly they respond and how clearly they know the mistakes they hope to avoid in the future.

In his memoir of a first pastorate, Rick Lischer tells about preaching "learned" sermons from full manuscripts to a salt-of-the-earth congregation of Illinois farmers. Shortly, Lischer reached "homiletical gridlock," a condition in which preacher and congregation meet each Sunday and ignore each other together. What's worse, no one told the young pastor that he wasn't relating to the hearts or souls of his flock, and he couldn't see it. Then, a fateful evening finally connected Lischer to a congregation heart-to-heart. A sick friend asked him to fill in one Sunday evening at Shiloh AME Church in East Alton, Illinois. It appeared to be an easy assignment—just preach the morning's sermon again. And, that's what Lischer set out to do until a saint in the second row recognized an out-of-touch preacher and prayed aloud, "Help him, Jesus." Other worshipers took up the cause with chants of "Make it plain! Preach! Come on up!" Something strange happened to Lischer. He realized proclaiming the good news is a conversation, an interactive exchange for both heads and hearts in a community. It was a revolutionary moment, a professional breakthrough, in a low-risk setting.[26]

We need opportunities to be novices before we have to solo in leadership. Usually before age thirty, we deal with four formative learning tasks:[27]

- Forming a life dream and giving it a place in our life's structure
- Forming mentor relationships
- Forming an occupation or calling
- Forming love and family relationships

COACHING CONVERSATION

Internships and volunteer service are expanding trends in the millennial generation, now graduating from college and moving into the workplace. Young leaders need places to practice leadership without threat. Service through our families, schools, churches, and communities provides formal and informal internships for us. Deliberate assessment is an asset for emerging leaders and for seasoned leaders as well.

Apocalyptic Surprises: Revelation and Rehabilitating Our Lives

The Book of Revelation was truly a tract for tough times, an apocalypse, or an "unveiling." Revelation redirected believers' lives from a negative crisis to positive encouragement. Written from a concentration camp and crafted in mystery and riddles, Revelation has caused many readers to redirect their lives and focus their leadership for more strategic outcomes.[28]

Golfers get "mulligans," the chance to hit another shot rather than settle for the results of the shot they just hit. Have you ever wanted a "do-over" with your life? Alfred Nobel decided he needed a mulligan in 1888 when he saw the headline over his premature obituary in the morning paper. His brother Ludvig had died in France, but the French newspaper assumed it was Alfred who had passed away and mistakenly announced, "The merchant of death is dead." Seeing what his legacy would be, Nobel decided to rehabilitate his life.

Nobel's father had been an industrialist in Sweden and Russia who succeeded in manufacturing explosives and machine tools. Alfred became a chemist, joined his father's business, and soon developed a safer way to make and stabilize nitroglycerin, a product he called dynamite. He invented detonators, blasting caps, blasting gelatin, and smokeless blasting powders. Alfred's financial gains from explosives and oil made him a very rich man. While he intended his explosives to be used for building tunnels, canals, roads, and railways, his reputation was actually much more negative. When he read that obituary summing up his life, he decided to refocus his legacy and resources. Upon his death in 1896, his will surprised his family and the general public. He left the bulk of his fortune in a trust to establish the Nobel Prizes. Alfred Nobel refocused his life from warfare to contributions to humanity. Like the Apollo 13 mission to the moon, Nobel was a "successful failure."

COACHING CONVERSATION

It's important to realize that it's never too late to recharge the aquifers of our lives. Leaders grow all their lives.

Interpreting the Text: Commentary on Leaders

Most religious leaders have biblical commentaries to help them understand the historic, linguistic, and comparative perspectives of the texts they're trying to understand for themselves and to frame for others. In a changing world, "leadership commentaries" are needed. The reason is simple. Leaders can't function with consistency and effectiveness without an overall theory or interpretation of leadership.

As you will see in chapters 2 and 3, I feel strongly that with the ebbing of the Industrial Age church leaders must adjust:

- It's time for congregational leaders to think in more biblical and contemporary terms, and in more organic terms, about how to lead living entities.

- It's time to affirm again that Christ's church is alive and best lead by organic processes.

In other words, it's time for an organic approach to be defined and described for faith community leaders. Taken together, our first three chapters create a dialogue about leaders, communities, and contexts from an organic perspective. This conversation draws us into aquifer-depth views of leadership.

✔ CASE STUDY: Matt's Soul Growth

Matt is a successful pastor. An exceptional student in college and seminary, he moved through the ranks of his denomination from smaller churches to larger ones. Along the way, Matt completed a doctorate, read and studied widely, and worked toward certification in pastoral counseling. His restless approach to learning kept him growing, stretching his self and soul. But, unlike many ministers at mid-life, Matt took a major risk. He launched into a new exploration of family systems' applications to congregational life. This approach made three concrete differences in Matt's practice of ministry: Family systems theory gave him a leadership framework, gave him a simplified cluster of actions to take as a leader, and lent him a growth channel for the long term. As a seasoned minister and leader, Matt found a way to grow his self and soul for life.

Tapping Aquifers of Self and Soul

The cluster of experiences we've examined so far tap into our aquifers of self and soul. Aquifers have some important qualities I didn't mention at the beginning of this chapter. Let me identify three that inform our leader growth processes.

1. Porosity. Aquifers hold water because the sands and rocks that make them up are porous and can be penetrated. These materials can absorb, hold, store, and conduct water.

COACHING CONVERSATION

We won't grow as leaders if we are impermeable and unable to let new things in. The more porous our selves and souls are, the more we will supply depth and refreshment to our communities.

---

2. Recharge areas. Aquifers can be pumped dry, but they can also gather new supplies of water in their basins or valleys. Recharge areas[29] are usually covered with vegetation and soil that filters and cleans pollutants from these new supplies of water. Hidden deep underground, aquifers supply groundwater for wells. Primarily under the plains of western Kansas, much of Nebraska, and the panhandles of Texas and Oklahoma, the porous rock formations of the Ogallala Aquifer provide water for the residents and crops of the region. Though invisible, this "lake" is vital to the area. These water resources are especially crucial now that irrigation has become a primary strategy for agriculture on the plains and, more importantly, now that the water tables of the aquifer have been drawn down. Recharging the deep water supply is a slow process. I'm told heavy snowmelts on the Eastern Divide of the Rockies take twenty-five years to work their way to the Ogallala Aquifer and raise its levels.

COACHING CONVERSATION

Leaders need new leases on life regularly. We are better served if those sources of new life are pure enough to sustain us.

---

3. Springs, artesian wells, and geysers. Sometimes aquifers pop out of the sides of hills as springs or newborn streams. On rare occasions, rock formations create pressure on water in aquifers. When wells are sunk into pressurized aquifers, water is pushed out without the aid of pumps. These overflowing wells are called "artesian."

A relative rarity, geysers are hot springs that erupt and can spew steam and hot water up to four hundred feet high. There are only about a thousand geysers on earth, and half of them are in Yellowstone National Park. The best-known geyser is Old Faithful, whose name describes its cycle of erupting every forty-five minutes. Like pressure cookers, geysers cook a mix of lots of water and intense heat in volatile pressure-tight underground basins.

COACHING CONVERSATION

Leaders do their work best when they can work out of the overflow. Explosions are spectacular to watch but impossible to contain.

New Seeds

"Sow and grow" begins with leaders. God uses a myriad of shaping experiences to deepen us, to provide spiritual aquifers for us. Think about your journey and its impact on you. We are not likely to be better leaders than we are persons. We are not likely to lead where we haven't been. Is God planting new seeds of leadership in you and me? The ultimate goal of all seeds is growth, maturity, and production. God is calling leaders for faith communities who are clear why they're here.

Now let's move to chapters 2 and 3 to explore how organic leaders relate to their faith communities and how they live in a world that's already in progress.

CHAPTER 2

Your Church Is Alive

Did you ever play the children's game in which you clasp your hands together with your fingers turned into your palms? You hold up your intertwined knuckles and say, "Here's the church." Then, you extend your forefingers upward together and say, "Here's the steeple." Finally, as you say, "open the doors," you rotate your hands so your fingers point up, and wiggle your fingers as you say, "and see all the people!" It was a good reminder that churches are people places, groups of living, breathing, believing volunteers. Good leaders look at congregations and see organic communities rather than organizations. Then they lead in organic fashion.

Living organisms are led differently than machines. That single fact creates a revolution in the way you and I lead our congregations. We're simultaneously leaving the mechanical mind-set behind as well as learning an organic approach to congregational leadership.

Oiling History's Hinges

The sea change from mechanical-to-organic thinking is magnified by a chasm in our world, causing massive brokenness. This great gulf grows out of our unique moment in world history. We live at the hinge of three contrasting mind-sets: the waning Industrial Age, the cresting Information Age, and the emerging Experience Age. Each of these points of view looks at reality in distinctly different ways. In many ways, the chasm is too wide, and these diverse perspectives are incompatible. Yet this hinge point is our arena for ministry and leadership, our opportunity to leaven human history.

The Industrial Age has lasted 300–400 years and is now waning. Scientific thinking dominated this era. Its mechanical assumptions gave us specialization, compartmentalization, and a reliance on "proof." In many ways, science took over theological thinking and became the unquestioned definition of reality.

Look at the denominations that have arisen from the Protestant Reformation–Baptists, Methodists, Lutherans, and Presbyterians, for example. Their structures are machine-like, and programs have dominated their ministries. This model fit the scientific world well until the middle of the twentieth century. Industrial congregations tried to be one-size-fits-all, full-service, multigenerational organizations, and many of them succeeded. They almost became "well-oiled machines." Then, competing mind-sets appeared on the scene. In response, some congregations majored only on one generation. Other congregations rushed headlong back to the past as they tried to recapture a simpler age. Neither of these approaches was willing to deal with the complexity of their world of ministry. Both missed God's offer of ministry.

The Information Age appeared in the 1970s and is expected to pass off the world scene as a predominant mind-set by 2020. This world grew out of the explosion of information sources–the Internet, cable television, e-mail, and the publication of ten thousand books each day. The Information Age exploded options and products, expanding marketing as a hot new art and science. In this new mix, congregations have discovered these information technologies and used them in ministry. Congregations share news and promotions electronically, create member networks with e-mail and pagers, and reach out to their larger communities by means of Web sites. Contemporary-styled churches have been especially comfortable with technology in worship and teaching.

Industrial Age and Information Age church members may sit side by side in their pews on Sunday, but they aren't fully comfortable with each other. Both believe in science and don't really question its assumptions, but they know something has changed. Their discomfort is more than mere generational differences. They grew up in different worlds. They have different definitions of reality. We moved from the "we" decade of the sixties to the "me" decade of the seventies to the "gimme" decade of the eighties without adjusting leadership approaches.

The Experience Age emerged in the final years of the twentieth century.[1] This brought a vastly dissimilar mind-set from its predecessors.

The Experience Age generation felt the rationality of the scientific world was too arid. They felt its insistence on proof was too cold and too distant. This mind-set demands direct experience, full participation, and immediate interaction with God. They are hungry for mystery, meaning, and memories–now. They want awe in their lives. They think in terms of communities and systems rather than individuals. The bedrock shift is from information to imagination. Unlike the industrial perspective, viewing life as a problem to be solved, the Experience Age sees life as a mystery to be savored.

Change's Speedometer

Note the speed of change. The Industrial Age lasted hundreds of years. The Information Age is estimated to be at mid-point already after its beginning in the 1970s. The Experience Age is well underway now but may pass off the scene before mid-century. A futurist mentioned to me that a transition now happens every fifteen or twenty years. Do you feel how fast our world is moving? "Ages" are shrinking from several centuries to a few decades. Our youngest leaders may deal with four or five massive changes of mind-sets during their ministries. That pace of change will stretch all of us. We will have to learn, unlearn, and relearn quickly to avoid becoming yesterday's obsolete leaders.

When the Industrial Age leaders bothered to consider systems, they referred to life as pinball games and acknowledged that organizational life had ricochets they couldn't plot scientifically. Maybe, as comedian George Carlin says, it's ironic that we seem to think technology can fix the messes we made by technology. Industrial Age leaders tried to understand the momentum of the pinball game but missed the obvious lesson: Communities are more like bodies than like pinball machines.[2] A fresh reading of the New Testament images of the body of Christ might have instructed them to have new eyes and see new approaches.

The Tide Has Turned

We have used mechanical maps to guide our leadership for more than a third of a millennium. The common advice has been to "find that, fix this, change that, apply leverage here." In the Industrial Age, leaders used machine images, mostly drawn from the pressure images of levers and hydraulics. Leadership was defined as "what you do," a series of programs, a set of skills, and the tricks of the trade. As the effectiveness of the mechanistic model has faded, trends, fads, and "flavors of the week" multiplied but still don't match our new ministry challenges.

Our cultural metaphors have been machine-like. We have even thought of our bodies as machines. But current thinking has shifted to talk about machines as bodies. Computers get viruses and self-heal. Pacemakers, replacement joints, man-made organs, and wet suits for swimmers patterned after sharkskin are common. "When metaphors change, it usually means that reality has done so already," observes Thomas Hine.[3]

Leaders are now beginning to discover organic approaches that fit living organisms. Leadership, in this world, is more about "who you are," art and craft, and processes for the faith community. The conversation has moved more to leaders than leadership, more to processes than programs, more to what's natural than manufactured, and more to what's lasting than the quick fix.

Happily for congregations, organic leadership is both ancient and future. Organic leadership is "old" with its roots in the Bible's insights about living things. On the other hand, organic leadership is "new," touching on the temper of our time as well as the hungers of our contemporary ministry settings. Living churches need lively leaders, and organic leadership meets that need. Organic leadership is sketching a new map to guide today's leaders.

FROM MACHINE MIND-SETS ←→ TO ORGANIC MIND-SETS

Lever/Gears to Bodies/Plants
Assembly Lines to Seedbeds
Compartmentalized to Interconnected
Science to Art
Monuments to Mysteries
Independence to Interdependence
Ends/Goals to Means/Pathways
Pyramids to Networks
Programs to Processes
Scientific to Systemic
Uniformity to Diversity
Lines/Angles to Spirals/Cycles
Analysis to Intuition
Reductionism to Holism
Inanimate to Living
Sequencing to Multitasking

Reading the New Testament Again...for the First Time

When the New Testament describes congregational life, it uses organic images. Yet, it's difficult to see churches as alive and spirited when we've worn our machine lenses so long. The picture is clear, however. Read the church images in the New Testament again. Challenge your eyes, and put organic lenses on deliberately—maybe for the first time. Read again about churches as families and flocks, parties and pilgrimages, citizens and holy nations, bodies and vines.

With new eyes, do you see the organic images of congregational leaders? Tenders of flocks. Keepers of vineyards. Heads of families. Bodies of Christ. Teachers of disciples. Guides for pilgrims. These aren't mechanical notions, are they? They depict living entities consistently. The lesson here is more than mere language or word pictures.

Images, metaphors, and language are pivotal for leadership practice. Why? The pictures we have in our heads are reflected in the words we use about leadership and the way we act as leaders. When the New Testament challenges us to "be transformed by the renewing of your mind" (Rom. 12:2), it calls us to fresh outlooks on our world and new words about that world.

Abraham Lincoln had it right for his time and for ours: "We must think anew, and act anew." What are the issues for renewing our minds? What if we "switched off" the traditional machine language we've long used for congregational life? What if we laid aside the leader-as-mechanic model? What if we instead used organic language to refresh our images of community leadership? What if we led as leader-gardeners? How would that change of mental model create new forms of leaders? Let's think and act anew.

I'm choosing to use "community" in this book to refer to church and congregational life. The use of a less routine word is deliberate. Maybe just the use of a different term will slow us or ever jar us into a livelier conversation about faith communities and the ways they are led best both theologically and practically.

How Leader-Gardeners Think: Seven Patterns

Today's leaders think about their opportunities differently. Industrial Age thinkers look at nature and see raw materials for manufacturing. It's a "take, make, waste" philosophy.[4] In contrast, organic thinkers from Information and Experiential Age perspectives look at nature and see models that can mentor us. While we know Christians are imitators of God's love (Eph. 5:1), we are also imitators of God's creation. Creation shows us what works and what lasts. Creation demonstrates patterns for leading living things.

You're entering a "New-Way-of-Leading Zone." It may seem a bit foreign to you at first. Don't worry. This chapter and later ones will help you understand and practice this simple guideline: Organic leaders learn from creation's examples. When leaders function as gardeners, here's how they think and act.

Leader-Gardeners Look at the "Big Picture"

Living organisms are more than the simple sum of their parts. Rather, they are whole systems. Our bodies include circulatory systems, digestive systems, and nervous systems. To see systems at work requires looking wide-angle, long-term, and big picture. You and I must develop a special kind of vision to see systems.

Remember the "cloud of witnesses" assurance in Hebrews 12:1? That image depicts a stadium filled with the faithful who have gone before us. They are invisible to most eyes, but they're cheering us on to victory. They are our unseen community of rooters. There's a big picture beyond the narrow context we're in.

The big picture unfolds itself in patterns. Recognizing these patterns involves

- *repetition,* because by definition patterns are recurrences of behaviors
- *mental distance,* because standing apart from our communities helps us see behavior more objectively
- *trusting our intuition,* believing that our values and instincts are sound
- *mystery,* a conviction that God will give us insight

The big picture lets leaders scout the future before they arrive there. They anticipate, consider implications, try to reduce surprises, and look over the horizon. To think strategically, leaders use systemic lenses to look at the world.

LEADER'S LEXICON

"Systems Thinking," a perspective that understands human life in families, congregations, and workplaces as connections and processes rather than parts and symptoms.

"Seeing" systems requires perspective, patience, and practice. We remind ourselves constantly to watch for processes beyond obvious symptoms, to wait to see what emerges, and to learn over time.

Leaders have to fight systems blindness.[5] Some of us are *space-impaired* and see parts rather than wholes, blind to the breadth of the system. Others of us are *time-impaired* and see the present without the past, blind to the history behind the current situation. Too many of us are *emotion-impaired*, missing the shaping factors our family's emotional systems have implanted in us.

Our families of origin are our best laboratories for experiencing and understanding relational systems. Often, the role we filled in our families of origin is the same role we'll play out in organizational life.[6] That's a handy insight for leaders. Are we acting like Daddy, or reacting to Momma? Are we the overresponsible firstborns, or the babies of the organizational family who want some slack cut for us?

Leader-Gardeners Observe the Flow of Processes

Living things constantly change and adapt. We are moving and morphing, always in process. Leaders learn to monitor "flow" rather than fixed moments, observe migrations more than moorings, and read processes more than "problems." This approach isn't an instant, "microwave-ready" solution. Don't forget that the "fullness of time" (Gal. 4:4, NRSV) referred to in the New Testament was a long time coming. The timing that led to Jesus coming to earth was a lengthy process of redemption.

Communities are always in conversation. In fact, leadership processes are conversations—guided and free-flowing—between communities and contexts, people and places. People in communities are constantly interacting, and leaders "host" those interactions.

Leader-Gardeners Fear Equilibrium

Communities crave stability and continuity amid change. But living things are at highest risk when we think we are most stable and most secure. What the prosperous Israelites of the Northern Kingdom failed to recognize was that being "at ease in Zion" (Am. 6:1, NRSV) was really pre-death. Perfect and permanent equilibrium only exists in graveyards.

COACHING CONVERSATION

Leaders challenge communities to stretch and move forward. Even though living communities try to adjust, they tend to automatically revert to past patterns. When the "steady state" of equilibrium is confronted, the system reacts and acts. Fresh vision and new options give communities opportunities to face being stuck.

Leader-Gardeners Move toward the Edge

Living organisms are most apt to change and "break through" on their boundaries. Margins, brinks, edges, and verges are where systems are most lively and most dynamic.

LEADER'S LEXICON

"Verge," the margin, boundary, border, or brink of something. A verge is the part of a system where change moves most quickly and where transition is most natural.

Think of the constant interactions of seas and coastlines. Imagine the "yeasty" relationships between neighborhoods and cultures. The edges of systems are literally on the verge of change.

COACHING CONVERSATION

"Living on the edge" doesn't sound very comfortable, but that's where the action is in community life. The edge is the arena in which balance is most frequently upset. The give-and-take of community life, especially the conversations between interest groups, diverse factions, and differing points of view, hammers out definition and direction. Often, we've thought of boundaries as defining what's inside and what's outside. Organic leaders understand that in living communities, edges are where new relationships grow.

Leader-Gardeners Flee Comfort Zones

Living entities are most lively when discomfort forces creativity. Necessity is, after all, the mother of invention. "Rubbing raw the sores of discontent" is an old formula for community change. Think of what persecution of the Christian believers did during the book of Acts; it scattered them and planted churches throughout the Roman Empire. In only one-third of a century, the early Christian movement spread like a prairie fire on the winds of persecution. Moving beyond our comfort zones is a sure-fire way to stir creativity and new ministries.

COACHING CONVERSATION

Unintended consequences make life more "interesting." We often set out to do one thing and discover we've triggered any number of second and third order changes. We toss one little pebble into a pond and create ripples that range far beyond the small splash we hoped to make. As leaders, we challenge ourselves to think, learn, and move beyond the familiar confines of our own comfort zones.

Leader-Gardeners Correct Courses on the Fly

With living organisms, no changes are simple. Each adjustment in a living community triggers unexpected changes. Surprises require responses. So leaders constantly do course corrections on the fly. Isn't it interesting to note how often Jesus' miracles and pivotal teachings happened "as he passed by"? Some of our favorite events and teachings from the Gospels may not have been on a "to do" list. God surprises us.

COACHING CONVERSATION

Making "mid-course corrections" became common language during the early space explorations. In those cases, astronauts adjusted flight paths in mid-orbit. In most cases, those carefully calibrated alterations worked well. With human systems, the need for correcting courses on the fly is constant but not always easy to calculate or to understand. Oshry observes correctly: "In organizations, much of the time we think we are dealing *person-to-person* when, in fact, we are dealing *context-to-context. And much that feels personal is not personal at all.*"[7]

Leader-Gardeners Give Structures Time to Emerge

Systems self-organize and structure themselves over time. Their patterns emerge uniquely and slowly. Mary, Jesus' mother, must have instinctively known this lesson, since she watched and thought carefully about the unfolding of Jesus' life and calling (Lk. 1–2, especially 2:51–52).

Watch communities shape their processes and pathways. When large-scale academic or corporate campuses are constructed these days, the sidewalks are often delayed—until the users have created their own walkways. Then, the paths are turned into sidewalks. Living things find their way. Leaders may be tempted to fix something before it's broken rather than harvesting things when they have ripened.

✔ CASE STUDY: Matt's New Way of Thinking

Matt's discovery of systems thinking changed the way he did ministry and leadership. He became more intentional about understanding the DNA of his congregation. Matt began to notice triangles, especially relationships that aren't directly accessible. He stopped focusing on surface symptoms and began concentrating on deeper processes. Matt used the past to consider possible futures. He quit making congregational change a test of wills. Most of all, systems thinking helped Matt to lead more calmly, knowing God's kingdom doesn't depend on him alone.

How Gardener-Leaders Act: Four Behaviors

Organic leaders do more than think strategically. They act in specific ways to relate to and lead living congregations.

Leader-Gardeners Plant Well

In creation, seeds and seedbeds interact for growth. When leaders think organically, they invest in the best seeds and plant lots and lots of them. They also create deep, fertile, receptive seedbeds for those quality seeds. Leader-gardeners plant their best seeds in their best seedbeds, creating the conditions for big harvests.

COACHING CONVERSATION

Seeds have the potential to grow. You and I didn't put that potential into the seeds. God did, and that means God's church deserves the best gardener, the best seedbed, and the best care to create a harvest worthy of God. Using the best seeds, in the best seedbeds, for best yields, is the best steward–ship. Leaders stay focused on those few most important initiatives that make for the best beginnings. Don't forget that most early growth is small-scale and happens underground where you can't see it. So, enjoy the mystery.

Leader-Gardeners Understand That Growth's Processes Are Self-reinforcing

Growth and health create their own momentum. They are self-reinforcing. Peter Senge correctly notes that "a living system builds itself."[8] Since God is Creator, those of us who believe in him "ally ourselves with life."[9] Biology describes living things as "self-making."[10] Health and production are God's norms. It's interesting to remember that Jesus' only "destructive" miracle was the cursing of the nonproductive fig tree (Mk. 11:12–14, 20–25).

COACHING CONVERSATION

Health generates energy naturally. If you as a leader are trying to will your community to change, you may be working against the natural energy of your own community.

Leader-Gardeners Carefully Cultivate Their Crops

In creation, all living things change, grow, relate, and adapt. Consequently, organic leaders focus primarily on two actions amid that ongoing flow of development: (1) planting prime seeds in prime seedbeds and (2) limiting nongrowth conditions. Good beginnings and reduced competition are keys to the harvest. As with good gardeners, "more seeds, fewer weeds" is the motto of the organic leader.

COACHING CONVERSATION

Gardeners cultivate. We weed out competing plants, leaving only the healthiest growth. We even thin our preferred plants when they are taking too much vital sunlight and nutrients from each other and begin interfering with growth and yield.

Leader-Gardeners Practice Seasonal Savvy

Creation contains seasonal rhythms of work and rest. We plan for the growing season and guarantee we plant well. We patiently await germination. We cultivate carefully and weed out the competition. We pray for warm sunshine and refreshing rain. We feed our plants with fertilizer and nutrients. We "lay by" the crop when it has grown too big to cultivate and wait for full maturity. We harvest our crop, storing seeds for the next season. Then, during the off-season, we begin to plan for the next growth cycle. See the biblical rhythms of intensity and rest in creation (Gen. 2:1–2)?

COACHING CONVERSATION

Intensity and respite are natural cycles in nature. In creation, God worked and then rested. Recognize the built-in oscillation of expenditure and rest. This "seasonal savvy" applies to communities and leaders.

Let the congregation expend its energies—that's a leader's stewardship. Then, help the community catch its breath as well—that's stewardship, too. Don't confuse summer and winter, fall and spring. These seasons serve different purposes and fulfill varied needs. Let the community recognize and enjoy the special qualities of each season for what it is and what it can be.

✔ CASE STUDY: Matt's New Way of Acting

Matt adopted an organic manner of leading. He worked on staying patient and growing himself. He tried to find multiple options for problem solving. He discovered his church's success wasn't about him. Matt coached his congregation's leaders to think and lead in more organic fashion. Matt's primary stewardship became self-growth, because he realized he would never lead his faith community where he had never been.

Organic Leaders as Immune Systems

What special function do organic leaders provide within their communities? Organic leaders serve as immune systems for the body of Christ.

LEADER'S LEXICON

"Immunity," the human body's protection against foreign invaders. Our immune system keeps us healthy and alive.

As leaders, we help our communities define ourselves, recognize who we are, and identify who may be invading us.

The community needs an immune response, to determine what is self and not self…The immune function, determining what does or does not benefit the congregation, is the task of leadership. Good leadership provides good immune functioning. Well before the practice of vaccination, physicians knew that people who had an infection once recovered more quickly if infected again. These people were said to have "wise blood." Similarly, healthy congregations develop an immune system. They do not permit pathogens to inflict harm on the community. Mature leaders give the congregation wise blood.[11]

- Immune systems *identify me and not-me*, us and not-us.
- Immune systems *protect me from not-me*, us from not-us.
- Immune systems *enhance me into me-plus*, us into us-plus.

Enhancing Immunity: Developing Wise Blood

Our human immune systems are combinations of barriers to guard against outside threats.

Our first barrier is "natural immunity" provided by our skins, acids in our stomachs, and other surfaces that repel invaders. These defenders are present from birth, are fairly nondiscriminating, and don't become more effective over time. They help us turn away or expel things that intend to harm us. From a congregational viewpoint, healthier births generally create healthier lives for faith communities. Our natural immunity serves us well when threats appear later in our ministries.

Our second barrier is "adaptive or acquired immunity" and responds to specific dangers. These responses can be strengthened. Immunity, from a leadership viewpoint, encourages health. How can we enhance our capacity to recognize and resist health threats?

- Immunity growth: the "vaccination" of experience. We become less susceptible to future attacks when we have survived earlier onslaughts.[12] Some doctors have reported that honey made from local pollens helps inoculate folks with allergic reactions to those pollens. The old saying that whatever doesn't kill us makes us stronger is true. It is no wonder C. S. Lewis described our faith as a good infection. Good experience is a godsend for leaders when outside pathogens try to invade.

- Immunity growth: our community. Relationships nourish us. Family and friends–even pets and plants–keep us going. Women's emphasis on building relationships may be why they live longer than men and why married men live longer than single men dealing with the same disease.

- Immunity growth: our practice of Sabbath. Rest, recreation, and renewal help us stay strong. In medical crises, induced comas are sometimes used to give our bodies time to recover. As a practical matter, leaders deal with crises better when rested and focused. The famed football coach, Vince Lombardi, had it right: fatigue makes cowards of us all.

- Immunity growth: nourishing our spirit and body. A healthy diet and supplements are regularly used to beef up and renew our physical bodies and brains.[13] One of the basic functions of discipleship and soul gardening is to grow us toward maturity in Christ and to give us clarity of identity in Christ's body. Congregations can be immunized against infections by providing a healthy diet for their spirits.

- Immunity growth: laughing, playing, and praying toward health. Stress lessens when we laugh and relax. Consider the case of Norman Cousins who, when in constant pain from a life-threatening tissue disease, laughed his way back to health?[14] Although doctors believed Cousins's 1964 ailment was irreversible, he found that watching Marx brothers' comedies triggered belly laughs that in turn allowed him an hour or more of pain-free sleep. Laughter exercises our lungs and circulatory systems and gets more oxygen into our blood. Laughing boosts endorphins, creation's painkillers in our brains. It's interesting that focus, passion, and a merry heart often make pain go away for a season. Leaders can learn a lot from the use of healthy humor during onslaughts and periods of high anxiety.

- Immunity growth: centering our souls. The Christian monks developed methods to reduce distractions and to center their souls on God. Some of those approaches are still used to focus our minds and bodies on the challenges of pain and apprehension. Clear focus, with few distractions, help leaders stay on track and on task when spiritual germs try to enter their community systems. Remember that "enthusiasm" means "possessed by God."

- Immunity growth: avoiding polluting elements. Breathing air filled with smog or with high ozone levels correlates with heart failure. Leaders need to keep pollutants out of their souls even more than their bodies.

- Immunity growth: donated immunity from transfusions and transplants. Sometimes we need others to come alongside us with resources we lack. No leader can afford to "go it alone." We're community-based beings. We need others' experiences, gifts, and strengths to function well.

Leaders are constantly placed in situations calling for all of their natural and acquired immunity. Work on enhancing your own spiritual and emotional immunity, because if you become infected, your sickness will spread to your community. Increase the immune response of your community, its capacity to identify and repel infectors.

A special category of immune response plagues congregations. We know it's tragic when our immune system overreacts, autoimmune responses occur, and our bodies attack themselves. We see this phenomenon in human disease when insulin-dependent diabetes, rheumatoid arthritis, and multiple sclerosis develop.[15] In congregations, we see fragmentation and disintegration when members become viral, turn on their own faith communities, and lose their ability to work for the mutual health of the body. In the end, viruses kill their hosts and, in effect, commit suicide. Congregational conflict often takes the form of internal attack and calls for leaders to provide immunity.

Organic Leadership: A Cultivation Process

Leaders as immune systems focus on three basic initiatives—common relationships, common faith, and common futures. As a result, organic leaders concentrate on three processes: connecting,

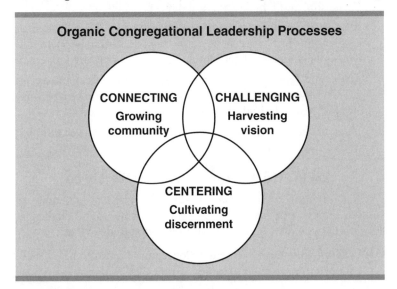

Organic Congregational Leadership Processes

CONNECTING
Growing
community

CHALLENGING
Harvesting
vision

CENTERING
Cultivating
discernment

centering, and challenging. Typical of organic or nonlinear thinking, there's no hard-and-fast order for the processes. Rather, the organic "order" moves toward the congregation's energy pools and allows leaders to strike when and where the iron is hot. Readiness is the magnet. Health is the incentive.

- *Connecting:* Leaders grow community. Without community, no leader has a constituency. Community, because it pivots on trust, is a shifting landscape. A new community emerges every time a new member joins the group or any time an old member drops out. Connecting is a basic ongoing organic leadership process.

- *Centering:* Leaders focus the community on discernment. The process of deliberately seeking God's will keeps the faith community rooted. Centering the community deepens spirituality and identity.

- *Challenging:* Leaders zero in on the community's future and harvest the fruits of vision. This ongoing process keeps the community new every day.

Practicing the Organic Model

Note several central characteristics about practicing this organic model of congregational leadership:

- *Energy:* The three functions of Connecting, Centering, and Challenging are verb forms. The processes of Connecting, Centering, and Challenging are never finished.

- *Interaction:* The three organic processes overlap. There is no first, second, third. They can be implemented simultaneously and usually need to be juggled simultaneously and blended together.

- *Movement:* They are circular processes rather than linear. As circles, they have maximum flexibility in implementation because circles "move" in both directions according to need.

- *Futures:* The three processes all have "-ing" endings, reminding us that the basic health issues of living things are ongoing.

How to Lead When You Don't Know What to Do

A good model for leadership guides us even when we're not sure what to do. Organic leaders always connect, center, and challenge. That's what you do when you're not sure what to do. Why?

- Leaders who have no connections have no community. Stay connected to your community. Connecting is ongoing because every change in your community's make-up refines your community. When a new member joins or when a current member exits, you have a new community that requires new connections. Remember that Jesus gathered an inner circle of disciples around him, leaned on friends such as Mary, Martha, and Lazarus, and kept an intimate relationship with God.

- Leaders who lose center lose credibility. Stay spiritually and emotionally calm to keep your anxiety from spooking you and others. "Calm and clear" is the key for leaders in pressure-cookers. Pray, take some deep breaths, define who you are, count to ten, refine your beliefs, call on objective persons for perspective, sleep on decisions, create quiet times, and follow Jesus' example. Review how he faced lake storms, walked through mobs that had him cornered, and stayed calm before Pilate.

- Leaders who aren't clear aren't challenging. Self-definition and self-differentiation are basic qualities for organic leaders. Before challenging others, leaders need to settle some identity questions. Who am I? What do I know to do? What do I believe? What are my strengths and gifts? What's my future? Fortified with crisp values, beliefs, and identity, leaders can then risk challenges to their communities. Revisit the "I am" statements of Jesus in John's Gospel for examples of self-identity and challenge.

Focus on three basic behaviors. Stay related. Stay calmly centered. Know who you are before you model change or ask anyone else to change. It's a simple formula, but it takes a lot of effort and energy to live it out in your community. We'll expand the organic principles and practices of connecting, centering, and challenging throughout the remainder of this book as "seeds of the future."

CHAPTER 3

Already in Progress

"Already in progress." You've heard the phrase while listening to your car radio or watching television, haven't you? The announcer prepares you for what comes next with a familiar introduction: "We now join our previously scheduled program already in progress." That announcement is good advice for living and leading as well as for listening. We're always "already in progress." Our worlds never stop. Our congregations are constantly changing. Church leaders are always dealing with moving targets. Some note that ministry contexts are changing. In truth, change itself is our leadership context.

Change Is Our Ministry Context

Living things change. Period. This truth is so obvious that it's not up for debate. If you're alive, change happens all the time. There's no stopping it. Although change in the natural world is never neat, predictable, or manageable, creation has always been "already in progress." God is at work, and leaders can join him in making a difference. In spite of this statement of faith, our Industrial Age mind-set has taught us to try to divide time into starts and stops. Scientific thinking has made us think of change in sequences, segments, compartments, lines, and angles. Machines are the images of organizations in the modern world. When machines break down, we identify the broken part, replace it, and gear up again. Start, stop, find, fix, and fire up are the change sequences for machines.

Churches Are Alive and Changing

In stark contrast to machines, congregations are living communities. That's the reason, try as we may, leaders and faith communities overreach when they announce they are "managing change." God built constant change into our universe and into our faith communities. Congregational transition is "already in progress." From a leadership perspective, congregational change isn't started or stopped by the will of congregational leaders. From a theological point of view, congregational change is by God's will and is the Creator's proprietary work. Congregations are called to become more like Christ, not more like their pastors. Congregational change is health-induced and persists in creation.

Just the same, leaders in the West generally want change on their own terms—fast, big, now. Churches typically mirror the larger culture in those expectations as well. I saw a bumper sticker that describes the styles of too many congregational leaders: "Let's do it my way. Then, let's do it my way again." When we adopt that point of view, constant change is still not enough. We want to engineer the change goals, determine the specific times, and set the pace with our own hands.

In change's unsteady march forward, creation uses an impressive array of paces. Sometimes natural change may be similar to a glacier, moving almost imperceptibly over long periods of time. Occasionally, change may occur like an avalanche when something snaps and there's sudden, localized, out-of-control slippage. Then, akin to the huge tectonic plates underpinning the continents, abrupt shifts may cause earthquakes with spectacular breakage. Creation chooses its own paces for change. Churches and other communities transition at different paces as well.

Creation's Turn Signals: Eight Lessons to Learn

Creation itself is a mentor about change for leaders and for congregations.[1] God built change into the world, and creation shows leaders a myriad of ways to deal with these natural transitions. Creation changes itself and points us toward understandings of transitions in ecosystems and solar systems, work and family systems, as well as multicultural and community systems. Leaders can learn from these basic lessons, those principles put on display by the Creator from page one of the Bible.

Creation Turns Corners by Finding the Easiest Contours

In creation, change follows paths of least resistance. Rivers and creeks meander downhill effortlessly. Creation doesn't "work" at change. Wheatley rightly observes, "Water answers to gravity, to downhill, to the call of the ocean."[2] Cattle and other animals climb mountains by finding the most gradual grades. In fact, before heavy-duty machines could move massive amounts of earth, road builders simply adopted cow paths for roadbeds and took the easy grades up inclines. The oldest roads followed ridges and valleys. They weren't as geometric or precise as many newer superhighway designs because they simply tracked the contours of the natural terrain.

COACHING CONVERSATION

Congregational leaders can learn a lot about change's pattern of following the easiest contours. Change builds its own momentum. When faith communities want change, leaders usually can't stop it. When faith communities don't want change, leaders usually can't force it. It's the contrast between easy climbs up slopes and scaling sheer rock faces by our fingernails. Take the easier contours. Go where there's already energy for change.

Creation Turns Corners by Overloading Itself

Change occurs naturally when a system is stretched beyond its breaking point. Wildfires, floods, hurricanes, tornadoes, avalanches, volcanoes, and intense storms leave their marks and change landscapes dramatically. A massive earthquake during the Old Testament era may have enlarged the Dead Sea (Gen. 19).[3] It's no accident that we remember Vesuvius, Mount St. Helens, the Galveston hurricane, the San Francisco earthquake, and the Johnstown flood. In all those cases, life was broken irrevocably and changed because nature overloaded itself. It's also no accident that, in the insurance business, these events are typically described as acts of God.

I grew up on a river bottom farm with an island in the stream. The island really didn't belong to our property. But, after some spring floods, the island was on "our" side of the small river. We gained or lost three or four extra acres of the island every time a flood washed a new channel in the river. There was really nothing we could do but accept the overwhelming, overloading power of flooding waters on Indian Creek in Southwest Missouri.

Tend to breaking points. Dramatic events—radical congregational growth, painful conflict, deaths of key leaders, damage to "sacred spaces," downsizing by major employers in a community—may fracture the faith community and become occasions for potential health, healing, and advance. Growth "appears from disequilibrium, not balance."[4] Brokenness is a leadership opportunity. Remember there's a theological response when the earth is broken, since the stewardship of the earth, the tending of God's garden, is man's oldest job (Gen. 1—2). The same guideline applies to God's communities.

Creation Turns Corners by Growing to Maturity

Living things are born small, but they change and grow toward maturity over time. As the parable of the mustard seed reminds us, "Though it is the smallest of all your seeds, yet when it grows, it is the largest of garden plants…, so that the birds of the air come and perch in its branches" (Mt. 13:32). The Japanese have a word, *nemawashi*,[5] for preparing roots for transplanting. The legendary Asian gardeners know it may take years to transplant a tree in ways that spare the plant the shock of being uprooted. Preparation for the next stage of growth is time-consuming but basic. Some snakes outgrow their skins, and some turtles shed their shells to grow to their next stage. Shedding and molting are natural processes in maturing.

Rooting believers in the foundations of faith and cultivating emerging leaders is critical to the future of any congregation. People and communities change when they mature and are ripened by experience. A young physician once sent me home to heal on my own without any medications. He patiently said, "In this case, we'll apply 'the tincture of time.'" The lesson was that time and patience frequently are all the healing force we need.

Creation Turns Corners by Hedging Its Bets

When nature reproduces, it spreads dozens, thousands, or even millions of seeds, spores, or sperm. One ordinary spruce cone has eighty seeds.[6] And a vole, a type of field mouse, produces seventeen litters of five every year–with the female babies ready to have their own litters when they reach one month in age.[7] Do the math. Creation leaves little to chance where the future is concerned, guaranteeing tomorrow by multiple seeds in multiple sites.

Take the case of dandelions. At best, dandelions are sources of salad greens from their leaves. At worst, they are troublesome weeds in our lawns. But in every case, dandelions are successful survivors. They hedge their bets by producing thousands of seeds from each little yellow blossom's "puff ball," winged seeds that ride the wind to other lawns. And, they don't leave their futures to seeds alone. A dandelion's taproot may penetrate three-to-six feet downward into soft soil. That's why slicing dandelions off at ground level rarely kills the plant. In fact, this common gardening maneuver may only encourage a new and hardier plant to sprout up. Think of how the dandelion guarantees its future. It multiplies from roots as well as seeds, and its seeds have wings! Dandelions may not be beautiful, but they are legendary survivors because they hedge their bets by sowing many seeds.

COACHING CONVERSATION

Industrial-styled leaders may put all of their eggs in one basket and risk their futures on one idea. But, they haven't learned the lessons of creation. Invest in lots of ideas and initiatives. Harvest the ones that flourish. Plant your best seeds in your best seedbeds, and trust God for the increase. Adopt the sincere roving Christian horticulturalist, Johnny Appleseed, as your change model. Born John Chapman, he planted untold numbers of apple seeds and trees on the frontier of the early 1800s, from Massachusetts to Michigan.

Creation Turns Corners When Seasons Change

Life has built-in rhythms, cycles that mark the flow of changes. Living organisms experience all four seasons and are always either finding life or moving toward death. We typically think spring and summer introduce new life, and then we expect fall and winter to bring dormancy or death. But, it's important to remember that life continues throughout every season. Winter weather may invite dormancy in trees and hibernation among animals, but these phenomena are actually sabbaticals or fallow periods when life rests up for another burst of growth when the season is more favorable.

Seasonal changes are eras of great opportunity, and terrible threats. Transitions open communities and systems either to greater health or deeper sickness, ushering in either demons or angels. Remember the incident when Jesus described healing from demons in terms of reaping and sowing? "...he who does not gather with me, scatters. When an evil spirit comes out of a man, it goes through arid places seeking rest and does not find it. Then it says, 'I will return to the house I have left.' When it arrives, it finds the house swept clean and put in order. Then it goes and takes seven other spirits more wicked than itself, and they go in and live there. And the final condition of that man is worse than the first" (Lk. 11:23b–26). Vacuums are dangerous in nature and in congregational life. Fill gaps in systems with angelic possibilities.

Creation Turns Corners by Healing and Self-renewal

Creation is busy repairing the chaos man has loosed. Cottonwood trees, planted in soil tainted by industrial mercury, clean the pollution. Polluted rivers are purified by aquatic plants. Our body's natural healing processes are mimicked to grow replacement tissues and organs. See the pattern?[8] Creation will teach us ways to be healthy, if we treat ourselves as living entities rather than as machines. God's creation has many lessons to teach us about healing and renewal for God's faithful.

At a cellular level, we're always renewing. Over a period of time, we literally are no longer our old selves. Human bodies are in the recycling business. Self-renewal may be most obvious in humans in the external changes to our skin, hair, and nails, but that's only the beginning. Skin cells die and are replaced every month, liver cells every six weeks, and brain cells every year.[9] Recycling is one of God's favorite ways of making all things new. When we're burned or injured, healing and scarring are outer signs of inner renewal.

Agriculture in the United States has been primarily monoculture, one specialized crop for each crop year. That approach contrasts with the prairies of the American Midwest, where the traditional grasses were mixed. In fact, four types of plants blended to create our prairies: cool season grasses, warm season grasses, legumes, and different kinds of sunflowers. There are now efforts to restore the traditional prairies by recreating the polycultures of natural grasses. Likewise, some are exploring farming approaches that use the wisdom of the blended prairie growth to feed our nation.[10]

COACHING CONVERSATION

Readiness wins. When a tree falls in the forest, leaving a space in the forest's canopy, what fills that vacancy? It's the tree or plant that's ready to take advantage of the gap. "First in" wins in this case. In creation, whatever's ripe gets harvested, whatever's prepared claims the vacuum. How is your congregation readying itself for whatever is next in God's will, the next renewal?

Creation Turns Corners by Teamwork

Creation requires teamwork out of necessity. When geese migrate, flying in their familiar "V" formation allows them to "draft" and travel 70 percent more efficiently than a single goose could. Interestingly, the role of flying at the point of the "V" is rotated. When the lead goose tires from the extra atmospheric resistance it encounters in the lead position, it falls back to the tail of the "V" and another goose moves to the point. Teamwork makes the migration of geese much easier.

COACHING CONVERSATION

Teamwork forms the foundation for volunteer communities. How is your congregation developing teams of leaders for the future? The New Testament emphasis on spiritual gifts demonstrates the blends and balances of strengths in the faith community. The rich array of gifts that God plants in congregations are there purposely: "so that the body of Christ may be built up until we all reach unity in the faith and in the knowledge of the Son of God and become mature, attaining to the whole measure of the fullness of Christ" (Eph. 4:12b–13).

Creation Turns Corners by Favoring Strength and Persistence

For centuries humans have watched and mapped the stars. Most of us probably consider our galaxy completed. But new research shows that our Milky Way is growing by swallowing up stars drawn from neighboring galaxies.[11] The strong gravitational pull of the Milky Way has stretched the smaller Sagittarius galaxy and is now adding stars to its mass by tearing Sagittarius apart. It's just a matter of which galaxy has the most powerful force of gravity.

One image of organic leaders is gravitational pull. Gravity draws everything to center and orients the entities it attracts. In the case of the Milky Way, it has apparently taken eons of steady pull to grow itself. Strength over time tilts the balance in its own direction. It's no wonder experienced farmers remind novices to "plow to the end of the row." Good ideas have their own gravity, their own centers. Michael Schrage identifies powerful ideas as "charismatic prototypes" and claims, "The prototype plays a more influential role in creating a team than teams do in creating prototypes."[12] Strong ideas pull other ideas to themselves.

Creation's Cascades of Transition

Living things are on the move, "already in progress." The wisdom literature of the Bible recognizes this pattern and notes that there's a season for everything under the sun. Then, it identifies fourteen of these specific "seasons." These times and timings help guide us through life's transitions:

a time to be born and a time to die,
a time to plant and a time to uproot,
a time to kill and a time to heal,
a time to tear down and a time to build,
a time to weep and a time to laugh,
a time to mourn and a time to dance,
a time to scatter stones and a time to gather them,
a time to embrace and a time to refrain,
a time to search and a time to give up,
a time to keep and a time to throw away,
a time to tear and a time to mend,
a time to be silent and a time to speak,
a time to love and a time to hate,
a time for war and a time for peace. (Eccl. 3:2–8)

Transition, our response to change, has its own patterns and prototypes, its own seasons and cascades.

Transition flows through three fairly predictable cascades:[13] endings, turnings, and beginnings.[14] Does it seem counterintuitive to describe changes as beginning with endings and ending with beginnings? Look at the process theologically. Think of the basic message of the New Testament. Before resurrection can occur, death must happen. This is the flow creation adopts to unfold its changes.

Endings: Away from the Old

The monks of early Christianity believed even their simple lives were too crowded to find the will of God. They deliberately made room for God to work and fill their lives. Wisely, they raised "ending" questions. What must we shed, lay aside, and leave behind to focus on God's will? What are we willing to let die in us to allow something new to grow in us? These are difficult, often painful, issues to face. Endings are necessary, but frequently uninvited and uncomfortable, occurrences in our lives.[15]

THE FUTURE BELONGS TO THE NEW.

Shaw Cunningham took me into his North Dallas garden, his pride and joy. A fig tree had overgrown itself and needed trimming. When Shaw finished his pruning work, my breath was almost taken away. He had cut the plant back dramatically. I looked at the stubby branches and told him, "You've killed it!" Shaw just smiled and reminded me of a rule of creation: Fruit only grows on new wood. His comment took me back in memory to my grandfather's apple orchard. It was a favorite day for me each fall when Grandpa pruned the deadwood out of the apple trees. I only went to the pruning for the bonfire, the spectacular conclusion of a day's branch removal. However, Grandpa knew he was doing strategic work. He was improving the next year's crop of apples by removing the nonproductive deadwood. For farmers and gardeners, pruning is an ongoing discipline. There are, after all, times for keeping and discarding (Eccl. 3:6b).

COACHING CONVERSATION

New growth is most dynamic. Streamline and focus community resources and structures on primary purposes. Deadness won't produce new life. Jesus stated this principle without hesitation: "my Father is the gardener. He cuts off every branch in me that bears no fruit, while every branch that does bear fruit he prunes so that it will be even more fruitful" (Jn. 15:1b-2). Maximum yield comes from the new.

LIVING THINGS NEED REST.

Trees and woody shrubs go dormant during winter. They become inactive and take "naps." Rest is essential in nature. Unfortunately, I must be dormancy-challenged. I've learned that lesson about myself from the fact that I've grown several bonsai trees to death. I know the word *bonsai* means "tree in a dish" in Japanese. I know these fragile plants are pruned to have small trunks, tiny limbs, and even restricted root systems. I know they are fed sparingly and watered with misters. I know all of these things, but I still want to see growth. I try to stretch the limits of the seasons, and, in the end, kill my bonsai from lack of rest. My compost bin contains several bonsai carcasses finally at rest. Living things observe cycles of rest because forced growth may weaken or even kill. The endings of fall and winter build toward healthy beginnings for the next spring and summer. There are times for birth and death (Eccl. 3:2).

COACHING CONVERSATION

Let the faith community catch its breath at regular intervals. The pattern of the Creation Story in Genesis reflecting work, rest, and worship is a model to imitate.

QUESTIONS FOR ENDINGS

- Can I abandon the familiar?
- Can I "put childish ways behind me" (1 Cor. 13:11)?
- Can I "loosen" my identity?
- Can I shed—or even kill off—the old?
- Can I close life chapters cleanly?
- Can I reinvest my worst-spent days?
- Can I leave behind pieces of my old life?

Turnings: Between Old and New

Once an ending unfolds, a "turning" can't be far behind. Turnings are those chaotic, uncharted "between" times.[16] Something has ended, but nothing has emerged and defined itself as the new reality yet. Although predictable and necessary, turnings are morale assassins. Like the Hebrews in the wilderness after their exodus from Egypt, nostalgia for what has been comes easily. It's always tempting to give up and try to reclaim what has already ended, but it's too late to recapture what has gone away.

Transitions-in-progress get messy. This "messy middle" is the killer of many of the plans we make. Simple transitions become more complex than we anticipated. Second and third order ripples spin out of the obvious changes we tried to make, exceed our expectations, and surprise us. These discoveries often discourage us; these uncertainties dampen our will to keep on until new beginnings are clear and claimed.

Leaders and churches are in jeopardy because our world is currently "between times." As we discover organic behaviors and thought patterns to replace outmoded ideas, we're in a turning. We're changing worldviews, and that's a chaotic process.

NATURE MOVES IN PATTERNS, BUT NOT IN CHAOS.

A friend of mine photographed the rock patterns in the bottom of mountain pools as a graduate school class assignment. He discovered something that's not apparent to the untrained eye of the casual observer. In the bottoms of mountain pools, stones work themselves to the center and create circular formations. Stones on the outer edges heave slowly into the middle, displacing those stones at the center. The lesson my friend drew from this phenomenon was that creation moves constantly but not chaotically. Rather, nature's motion is patterned, reflecting "strange attractors."[17] Ecclesiastes had it right: There are times for scattering stones and other times for gathering them (Eccl. 3:5a).

COACHING CONVERSATION

Avoid organizing ministries to death. Keep these efforts on track without wasting lots of time and effort on structures that may stifle.

WHEN CREATION'S MOVEMENTS ARE TOO STEADY, WE MAY BE BLINDED.

We know ocean tides are restless, always ebbing and flowing. Most tidal ranges (the difference between low and high tides) are just a matter of a few feet. However, in the bathtub-shaped Bay of Fundy— between Maine and New Brunswick to the west, and Nova Scotia to the east—tidal ranges are the most dramatic in the world. Here the tidal ranges vary from thirty to fifty-two feet! Boats are tied with extremely long mooring ropes so they can bob along on high tide and still rest on the bay floor during low tide. The force of incoming tides on the rivers feeding into the Bay creates "tidal bores," swirls of water moving with so much momentum that they whistle aloud. These twice-each-day occurrences are extremely impressive, especially to visitors. Yet natives tend to take all this energy for granted. In fact, these strong tides, potentially the world's greatest natural source of hydroelectric power, were not harnessed for power generation until

1984. The reason is simple: Continuous change blinds us to options. Sometimes we need to keep searching rather than giving up (Eccl. 3:6a). When movement is unrelenting, we may become blind to possibilities.

COACHING CONVERSATION

Humans find it nearly impossible to see the unfamiliar while looking at the familiar. That includes leaders. Don't let yourself be hypnotized by the rhythms of activity. Be alert for potential in the natural momentum of change.

QUESTIONS FOR TURNING

• Can I surrender to "the gap" and ride out the "muddle of the middle"?

• Can I live with ambiguity's "shades of gray" and give God time to clear my head?

• Can I allow chaos and formlessness to grow into a God-shaped life?

• Can I find the patience to wait on God?

• Can I learn the lessons of "half time"?

Beginnings: Toward the Next

At last transition delivers us to a new beginning. The "next" has arrived. And, it's high time. We know turnings, those loops in our life journey, may be acceptable for a visit, but we wouldn't want to live there. We're ready to move ahead. We're ready for visions and maps.

MAKE A GOOD START.

As I mentioned, I grew up on a farm. Growing things is second nature. Drop a seed into the ground, and something recognizable sprouts automatically. Right? Not quite. Even the simple process of growing a lawn became a challenge when I moved to Richmond, Virginia. Every spring I'd plant, water, fertilize, and pamper Kentucky 31 fescue. Then I'd watch the shoots of grass flourish for a while before they died in the heat of summer. After a couple of years of frustration and failure, I enrolled in Virginia Tech's Master Gardener Program, a group of volunteers who coach folks who are as unsuccessful at growing things as I'd become. In that training program I learned the secrets of turf grass in Central Virginia. Our soil is the sandy, salty leftovers from the ancient seabed's retreat to the

Chesapeake Bay. Such soil isn't hospitable to some plants, like the fescue grass I'd sown in my yard. The Master Gardeners taught me the "SOD" method. Plant, water, fertilize, and pamper fescue's shoots during September, October, and December (SOD) to grow a root system. Then, when spring arrives and the grass begins to grow again, it already has a strong root network that withstands July's heat. It turns out that growing a lawn is a fairly simple process: because turf grass will either grow roots or shoots, invest early in depth to gain height. Good beginnings make for better futures.

COACHING CONVERSATION

Concentrate on the durability of good root systems. Like any firm foundation, early strength and stability allow for later growth.

TAKE THE RISKS OF PLANTING WELL.

Most healthy trees have a root system that's three times the diameter of their canopy of branches and leaves. One exception to that rule occurs when "container conscious" saplings or shrubs are planted with no challenge to their limited root systems.

Several Januarys ago, we had a terrible ice storm here in Richmond. It literally took me three days to get home from Williamsburg, usually only an hour's drive. When I was finally safely in my house, I stood at the front window of my family room and surveyed the frozen landscape. A snowplow hurtled down my street, using its momentum to break up and hurl hunks of ice onto the lawns. A small evergreen shrub by my driveway was hit by one of the ice chunks and rolled upside down onto the icy lawn.

I rushed to its aid, but I was too late…by fifteen years. I discovered this little shrub had become container conscious in its earliest days. It probably had been left too long in a plastic bucket at the nursery where its roots had extended out to the plastic barrier. Blocked from any additional growth outward, it had assumed the world was no larger than an eight-inch bucket and had settled for growing around and around. I imagine the developer who built my house needed lots of plantings for all of the houses he was building at the time, and the nurseryman made him an offer he couldn't refuse. Supplied with a truckload of little evergreens, he had planted these stunted shrubs without any preparation of the plant.

The problem with container conscious plantings is that they don't extend their root systems out to gather the nutrients and water needed for full health. To help them regain health, those tightly bound circles of roots need to be cut apart and spread out when the shrub is planted. It may seem like a brutal procedure. But, healthy growth calls for taking the risks of pulling the root ball apart drastically to create a larger arena. Ecclesiastes has it exactly right: there are times for planting and times for uprooting (Eccl. 3:2b).

COACHING CONVERSATION

There's a lot of wisdom in the warning of nurserymen: don't plant a fifty dollar tree in a fifty cent hole. Make a good beginning. Prepare for growth from the earliest stages of planning and planting. Plant well. Beginnings are critical.

QUESTIONS FOR BEGINNINGS

- Can I discern early hints of new directions?
- Can I enjoy the journey as much as the destination?
- Can I live with the process and let God take care of the product?
- Can I claim and act on new destinies?
- Can I attend to the movements of God?
- Can I begin again?

Change Is in the Air

A comedian once claimed that change is inevitable, except from vending machines! It's true that in the living world, creation is always "already in progress."

Because change is ever with us in community life, how do leaders relate to it best? How do organic leaders plant and cultivate the seeds of new futures? Given that creation is already in progress, what can leaders do or try to do amid changing systems?

First, think of changes you're involved in now. How many of the ways creation turns corners apply to your situation? How can you add natural momentum to what creation is doing already?

Second, given the changes you've identified, which of the cascades of change—endings, turnings, and beginnings—apply to the phases of your change situations?

You were introduced to an organic leadership model in the previous chapter. This approach weaves the processes of connecting, centering, and challenging together. Applying the organic model, let me suggest three concrete change initiatives for community leaders.[18]

1. **Connecting to Changing Communities:** Change naturally flows out of the life of faith communities. Leaders connect to their communities, recognizing that disconnected leaders have little ability to hear or articulate the deepest yearnings of their communities. Getting connected and staying linked gives ears to hear and a voice that's also heard. Healthy relationships open doors for change. After all, change is health-induced.

2. **Centering for Changing Communities:** Faith is dynamic, a lifelong experience of discerning God's will both personally and corporately in our faith communities. Creating processes that deepen our relationship with God as well as using disciplines that stretch our faith are foundational leadership initiatives. A healthy core leads us toward change. Remember that change is health-induced.

3. **Challenging for Changing Communities:** Communities are unlikely to magnify their vision, extend their reach, or enrich their ministries without leadership. Calm challenge and heartening courage offer a platform for risk-taking and advance. When leaders model "heart" for their communities, change becomes much more likely. It's a simple principle: Change is health-induced.

Change Communities and Community Change

For communities to move toward healthy change, they become health-oriented change communities. Think of community change as processes with three interlocking roles: sponsors, change agents, and advocates. As health is pursued in communities, leaders help the community remain connected, centered, and challenged. In particular, leaders invite the community's key sponsors, change agents, and advocates into constant conversation.[19] Community leaders believe in the "wisdom of crowds."[20] They are confident that *many* members are more discerning than the *few,* and that God's future is more often found in the best rather than the merely good.

- Every change has to be sown and sponsored. Someone cultivates the seeds. Congregational leaders can serve as sponsors of change. However, if the faith community itself assumes the sponsor role, change is automatically made legitimate and draws needed resources more easily.
- In centered faith communities, specifically in churches with congregational polity,[21] God becomes the change agent. Leaders

may teach, advise, facilitate processes and meetings, and coach persons and progress, but God remains the ultimate catalyst for the future. As the Scripture affirms, God gives the harvest (1 Cor. 3:6–9).

• Ideas and projects need advocates, leaders with passion and patience in the face of resistance and sabotage. Advocates learn to do new things in old ways and old things in new ways to keep change related to what's near and dear to the larger community.

✔ CASE STUDY: Matt and Change

Matt's systemic view of congregational life altered his view of change. Early in his ministry, he tried to "manage change." He practiced manual, hands-on ministry and found himself overworked and stressed. Then he realized change is built-in and cascades on its own. Nothing stays as it was, including churches. Matt relaxed and started fanning the flames God had already stoked in the life of the congregation. He discovered that his ministry context wasn't changing. Change *is* the context.

Creation and Culture

Our churches are "already in progress." Organic leaders grow throughout our lives and learn from creation. We respond to the

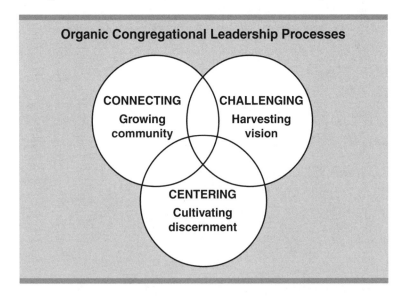

Organic Congregational Leadership Processes

CONNECTING
Growing community

CHALLENGING
Harvesting vision

CENTERING
Cultivating discernment

cultural hungers of our ministry arenas. We are always connecting, centering, and challenging our communities.

Now we apply our model of organic leadership and begin to enrich our practice of being lively leaders for living churches.

PART 2

Growing Communities, Calling, and Courage

Creation mastered chaos and gave us land, water, and sun. These are basic elements for organic leadership. Land, water, and sun metaphors provide raw materials for Organic Leadership 101.

The land folds into watersheds to gather, collect, and pool water into liquid communities–rivers, bays, and oceans. Leaders grow communities, those gathering points and meeting places for people. Leaders plant connections.

Influenced by the power of gravity, the waters themselves take on many natural shapes. Picture watery, gravity-molded shapes: ocean waves, clusters of clouds, and infinite varieties of snowflakes; raindrops, dewdrops, and teardrops; snow crystals, sleet pellets, and icebergs. Leaders cultivate centers of gravity, providing spiritual and emotional depth for themselves and for their communities.

The sun warms us, cheers us, and attracts us to face it for growth. Growth from our power sources takes on its own momentum and moves forward. Leaders focus future challenges from power sources and courage.

Creation links all of its elements together. The land, water, and sun interact constantly. After the Asian tsunami on December 26, 2004, the water level in a deep well in Blacksburg, Virginia, temporarily rose seven feet. Through brokenness inside the earth's crust, water's movements snaked through underground labyrinths to change water levels in a well a half-world away. Creation is connected. Organic leaders remember and practice that pattern.

In faith communities, organic leadership pools into a basic triad. Organic leadership weaves three relational processes together–connecting, centering, challenging. Taken together, they grow into faith communities of consequence. However, typical of living things, connecting, centering, and challenging appear and move in no set order. The ebb and flow of your community's energy will signal you what needs to be drawn into the foreground for it's the community's own health and future.

The next three chapters explore the practice of our organic model of leadership element by element:

- Connecting 101: Growing Community Breadth
- Centering 101: Growing Community Depth
- Challenging 101: Growing Community Height

CHAPTER 4

Connecting 101

Growing Community Breadth

I learned a painful leadership lesson one afternoon marching at the head of a military drill column. It was a bitterly cold and windy winter day, and I was the "leader," the soldier at the front end of a line of marchers. Walking into the teeth of the gale, I didn't hear a command to stop and reverse direction. So, I trudged on and on. I saw a chain-link fence looming up and hoped for some instructions before I collided with it. I got those orders loud and clear when the drill sergeant ran to my side and, in no uncertain terms, told me to stop. Then, he predicted my eternal destiny and said a number of other things I considered too blunt for civilized conversation with a nice Baptist boy. When I looked back across the field at my column and saw them laughing at my predicament, I realized I was no longer their leader. Without a connection to those guys, I was just out for a very cold walk into a wintry wind.

No Community, No Leaders

Without a community, there are no leaders. In leadership history, the "Great Man" theory was the first major concept of how leaders succeeded. In short, these unusual persons were in the right place at the right time to seize their moment in history in heroic fashion. The implication is simple: Leaders are everything, and communities are nothing. But, when leadership became a formal research pursuit last century, two primary types of leaders and one huge lesson about communities were identified:

- appointed leaders are selected by their groups for a specific role
  or
- emergent leaders rise spontaneously from within the ranks of their groups.

No matter which route we take to leadership roles, the community is required to bless and to join us. No community, no leaders. It's just as simple as that. Leaders lead from the inside of our communities. We get connected and stay connected.

So how are connections made and communities formed? What gathers communities together? Obviously, there are lots of ways by which groups of people find other kindred spirits and common causes. But, at its base, growing our leadership community calls for relationships of friendship and trust. In this chapter, we'll concentrate on only three community-building actions:

- befriending people,
- seeding trust, and
- understanding families of origin.

These basic leadership watersheds grow community.

Watersheds: Drawing Community Together

Watersheds[1] are geographic areas draining to a common waterway, a stream, lake, estuary, wetland, and ultimately an ocean. Numerous sub-watersheds combine into interconnected webs of water on the move.

LEADER'S LEXICON

"Watershed," an area drained by a waterway, and, in this case, a metaphor for community.

I live in the Chesapeake Bay watershed, funneling precipitation from Virginia, New York, Pennsylvania, Maryland, Delaware, and West Virginia as well as the District of Columbia into the Bay. Watersheds collect precipitation from higher elevations to move it into common bodies of water downstream. They also sink precipitation into groundwater stores.

It's generally easy to identify a watershed's boundaries. The most obvious natural watersheds in America are along its eastern and western mountain ranges. Watersheds define how precipitation of all kinds is gathered and channeled. Have you noticed that watersheds are now identified with signs along our interstates? The dividing effects of watersheds are obvious, since they are turning points for runoff. But, consider the multiplying and consolidating force of watersheds.

The Big Run Basin in Virginia's Shenandoah National Park is situated between Rocky Top Ridge and Rocky Mountain. It's a small area, relatively speaking. Yet even at only eleven square miles, it's still the largest watershed in the park. Here's the impressive multiplying factor. When one inch of rain falls into Big Run Basin, the runoff translates into two hundred million gallons of water downstream in the Shenandoah and Potomac Rivers and on into the Chesapeake Bay. Think of it. One inch of rain turns into two hundred million gallons of runoff!

Likewise, in person-to-person communities, one person's influence and effort pools and adds up. Like nature's watersheds, community multiplies its impact as well when friendship webs expand and trust deepens. Theologically speaking, congregations are "we-with" communities. We are in partnership with God and in faith networks with other believers. The New Testament, mostly in Paul's writings, cites forty-five "we-with" connections.[2] We live and die with God (2 Cor. 7:3). We suffer with God (Rom. 8:17). We are crucified with God (Rom. 6:6). We are raised with God (Eph. 2:6). "We-with" relationships are our theological prototype for connecting.

Reframing Our Field

Organic leaders focus on three basic fields of action: connecting, centering, and challenging. These three actions, woven together, enhance the influence of communities. Let's preview our model:

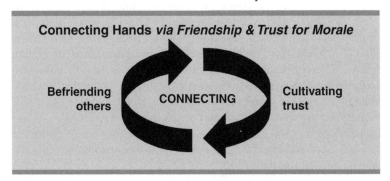

Connecting Hands *via Friendship & Trust for Morale*

Befriending others   CONNECTING   **Cultivating trust**

In nature, three kinds of relational communities form. Each is a type of watershed.

- Taker-Giver communities are parasitic.[3] These relationships draw life from others, called hosts, and create "win-lose" groups. Parasitic churches are prone to fragmentation.

- User-Neutral communities are considered "commensal." In these communities, one party benefits, and the other party neither gains nor suffers. Scavengers are examples of commensalism and demonstrate these "win-tie" linkages.[4] Scavenger churches are private fiefdoms existing for one or a few members.

- Partner-Ally relationships provide the most attractive communities for humans with free will and initiative. These groups grow mutualism, symbiosis, and "win-win" connections.[5] Mutual churches create real community. Community is God's way of multiplying us and making us stronger for leadership and ministry purposes.

While congregations can be found that reflect all three of these patterns, in church life as well as in creation, mutualism grows a better today and a more positive tomorrow for churches. The relationships that emerge from Partner-Ally links are founded on connections of friendship and trust.

Growing Leaders for Communities: Streams of Friendship

From a connecting point of view, how do leaders make friends and form communities? A friend, a professional fundraiser, reframed friendship for me recently. I asked him how fundraising was going for him. He answered that he did "friend raising," not fundraising. His explanation was that funding followed friendship. I think he's exactly right. Our treasures show where we put our trust (Mt. 6:21).

Our communities shape us. If you grew up in a small, high trust, family-oriented church like the Olivet Presbyterian Church in Staunton, Virginia, it's likely the larger congregation treated you like family. Church members may have even disciplined you when you forgot to be reverent. That's the story Don Reid of the Statler Brothers' singing group tells about the church of his childhood. He claims," I still can't grow hair on that spot on top of my head where Elmer Sensabaugh thumped me."[6] You have community when members feel so connected to each other that responsibility and discipline are shared throughout the group.

Although growing community isn't easy, the power of social networks is crucial in America.[7] Especially among mainstream Protestants, we are no longer automatic "joiners," no longer attending church in such high numbers, and no longer giving to charities as generously. Watching television, waning volunteer availability due to two-career families, and urban sprawl have all been blamed, rightly or wrongly, for the loss of social capital.[8] Growing communities requires "face time," and that time is becoming scarcer in our more impersonal era.

COACHING CONVERSATION

Most of us belong to more than one community. And those communities tend to be more open than closed, more flexible than fixed. In some quarters, communities try to shut out people and ideas. Those attitudes are apt to be unsuccessful and unhappy. Our world is too interactive and too oriented to group diversity to foster a one-size-fits-all style of community life.

Whom Do You Love?

The Bible asks us to identify our neighbors (Lk. 10:29). In fact, we show who we consider our neighbors to be by our friendly behaviors. Four basic behavior patterns are obvious in research on how friendships form:[9]

WE LIKE THOSE WHO "LIKE US" AND SAY SO.

It's natural, isn't it? When we sense someone likes us, enjoys our company, and gives us signals that they like us, we like them right back. Mutual admiration societies draw people together.

WE LIKE THOSE WHO "ARE LIKE US" AND SHARE OUR BELIEFS AND ATTITUDES.

"Birds of a feather" do flock together, don't they? Common history, values, and experiences tie us together. Jargon, acronyms, inside jokes, and information we take for granted show insider perspectives in community life. In such circumstances, we assume everyone thinks and acts just like we do.

WE LIKE THOSE WHO "ARE WITH US" AND EASE OUR LONELINESS AND PAIN.

Sometimes one moment in time generates a long-term friendship for us. Tom Conlon and I have known each other since 1971. We became friends almost instantly the first time we met. We spent a long August night pacing in the waiting room of a maternity ward in Lawrence, Kansas. Our wives were both delivering babies, and both were having difficulties. Because fathers weren't allowed access to delivery rooms in that era, we waited, walked, talked, and bonded. We learned to talk walking away from each other and walking toward each other as we crisscrossed the waiting room. Firstborns Cass and Kathleen were born healthy, but unhappy, early the next morning. For the next couple of years until both families moved eastward, our parts of the Conlon and Dale families met every twelfth of the month to celebrate another "birthday" and spin yarns about what each of our babies had done or could do. On those occasions, Tom and I had special stories or unique memories of that night we met and became friends. We were there for each other during one of life's "dark and stormy" nights. That forged a friendship for us.

WE LIKE THOSE WHO ARE "NEAR US" AND MOVE IN CLOSE PROXIMITY TO US.

Proximity plays a role in friendships. The old adage that "absence makes the heart grow fonder" isn't always true. Can you remember a best friend from childhood or school days or a workplace, a person you confided in and trusted then, but no longer have ties to now? If you no longer relate to such a special friend, it may be that distance is a factor in the loss.

I've already mentioned my 1992 experience of donating bone marrow for my next younger brother. Although we had many of the same interests and shared experiences as children, we had spent almost no time together for a third of a century. Our lives had moved in different directions. I left for college and moved progressively eastward. He moved west, went to college, settled into jobs, and established his family. We were together for brief periods of time at large-scale family gatherings, but stayed in touch mostly through occasional phone calls. We hadn't been in each other's homes more than five or six times in thirty years. I assumed he was markedly different from me, and he apparently had reached the same conclusion. When the extended hospitalization occurred, we got reacquainted. To our surprise, we discovered we were two peas in a pod. We thought alike, had common values, and made decisions in similar ways. Plus, we had a bone marrow match like twins. Distance had divided us more than any real differences.

Friendship is fueled in mysterious ways, by good chemistry and commonalities. Accept old friends as gifts from God. Cultivate new ones for today and tomorrow.

Cues and Clues for Community

Leaders of faith communities connect and reconnect. We grow emotional connections with and to our community from our first day in the group. We follow the instructions of Paul: "Practice hospitality… Rejoice with those who rejoice; mourn with those who mourn" (Rom. 12:13b, 15). We get to know people, and we demonstrate care for them. We concentrate on one-to-one and one-to-a-few relationships, but we also look for ways to create a sense of intimacy in one-to-many settings.

As we spend more time in a community, we squelch the impulse to assume we're automatically in relationship with others. Rather, we work at staying connected. We emphasize accessibility and "face time." We take part in life rituals—baptisms, weddings, funerals, and other passages—when family systems are especially receptive to old and new connections. Inevitably, connections are strained or broken. Then, we have opportunities to repair relationships. We may apologize for mistakes. We may admit our weaknesses and try to do better. We may agree to disagree agreeably—and make a good faith effort to grow new and sturdier relationships. Then, when enemies become friends, God has healed the enmity and distance.

Friendships are mysteries filled with cues and clues. Connections are embodied and incarnated. "The Word became flesh and lived for a while among us. We have seen his glory…" (Jn. 1:14a). Some relational signals are overt, verbal, and visible. Others are subterranean, silent, and invisible. In fact, more than 90 percent of human communication is nonverbal and symbolic. Hints from our eyes, from body language, and from relational spacing are streambeds for our communities, gathering and guiding our connections.

Connecting with Our Friends

With our friends, the "eyes" have it. Our eyes tell much of our community's story. Eye contact creates rapport and signals that we are present in the relationship. In Anglo culture in the United States, staring generally isn't acceptable, even among friends. If same-gender persons stare at each other, aggressiveness may be communicated. When different-gender persons stare, seduction may be sensed. In spite of the risks and nuances, we still look at each other for clues to our friendship, its boundaries, and its communication progress. As a rule of thumb, we look at our companions about one-third of the time when we're talking to them and about two-thirds of the time when we're listening to them.

We know our eyes blink regularly to cleanse their surfaces. But, our eyes also blink involuntarily when our brain recognizes the ends of paragraphs and ideas. That pattern makes a fast eye blink rate a cue to intense concentration. Rapid blinking signals observers that the other's internal computer is running. Good communicators wait until the thinking process has reached the end of an idea before adding more information into the mix. Cues like eye blinks help us listen for the "music" behind the words.

COACHING CONVERSATION

Look at other people, especially friends. Yogi Berra was right. You can observe a lot "just by watching." Keep your eyes open, and watch others' eyes for connections.

Body Language and Friendship

Our bodies "talk," too. Body posture can hint at whether people are open or closed to relating. Even when we aren't deliberately reading cues from others, our brains and intuitions are applying emotional radar to others and interpreting covert messages all the time.

Some of us have the gift of communicating beyond words. Those who are gifted at cultivating relationships are called "Connectors,"[10] and are in synchrony with people with whom they relate. They instinctively mirror the body language, vocal rhythms, and facial expressions of the person with whom they're interacting. As a result, the others typically respond positively to Connectors and like them. They *should* like Connectors, since they're seeing *themselves* reflected in Connectors.

COACHING CONVERSATION

Friends generally share a level of trust. That special connection buoys and moves them toward deeper waters.

Inner Space and Outer Space

Humans feel we have our own spaces in the universe, sometimes described as "body bubbles." These spaces extend several paces behind our bodies, an arm's length or less to our sides, and at varying lengths to the front of us. Consequently, we are wary of folks who are behind us, where we can't see what they're doing. Our body bubbles don't extend very far to our sides, however. We are generally more comfortable sitting in churches or theaters almost shoulder-to-shoulder with people we don't know.

Our "space" needs are fairly predictable. "Public space" extends beyond twelve feet or so; this person-to-person space is live-and-let-live distance where no direct interaction is expected. We notice people at a distance but can essentially ignore them. If we're approaching another person on a sidewalk, at about twelve feet we acknowledge the other person by glancing away or "dimming our lights." Face-to-face distance is "social space" from four to twelve feet and calls for give-and-take. Networking and most friendly exchanges happen within social space. Our closest relationships occur in "intimate space," inside a range of two feet or less. This "up close and personal" dimension of our body bubbles is reserved for those few people who are most special to us.

COACHING CONVERSATION

Become your own research project. Note how you use space. Sense when you feel comfortable, crowded, or connected. Learn from yourself as a test case, since other folks probably experience the world in similar ways.

Growing Communities through Leadership: Pools of Trust

Life's first lesson is trust, according to Erik Erikson.[11] As infants, we learn either to trust or mistrust. When trust is present, consequently, it becomes the gravitational force for community life and the watershed that propels it to greater depth. Our community may be two people or two thousand souls. The size of the community isn't the key variable—as long as trust is present. But, trust's messages and embodiments have to remain consistent no matter how many folks are related.

- One-to-one: "I have faith in you!"
- One-to-a-few: "We can rely on each other!"
- One-to-many: "We aren't anxious about what will happen here!"

Trust is a "good experience" phenomenon. I trust you if my experience with you has shown you to be trustworthy, literally worthy of my trust. It takes time and positive history for trust to evolve.

Having common experiences and holding things "in common" builds community and feeds trust in groups. Think of trust in this sample A-B-C-D-E order:

- A—Affinities, or common interests, stimulate trust.
- B—Backgrounds, or common heritage, provide a touchstone for trust.
- C—Causes, or common visions, invigorate allegiance and trust.
- D—Debris, or common wounds, form instant communities of experience and trust.
- E—Experiences, or occurrences in common, are platforms for trust.

The rich array of "common" items or experiences literally goes from A to Z.

COACHING CONVERSATION

Communities, by definition, hold things in common. Commonality is one of the basic watersheds for trust. Remember what happened after the community experienced Pentecost? "All the believers were together and had everything in common. Selling their possessions and goods, they gave to anyone as he had need. Every day they continued to meet together in the temple courts. They broke bread in their homes and ate together with glad and sincere hearts, praising God and enjoying the favor of all the people" (Acts 2:44–47a).

Joe and Jane Trust

Trust isn't theoretical or impersonal. It always has a "face," a name, a history, and a persona we recognize and appreciate. Look at some primary contours for trust's "identity" below.

WE TRUST LEADERS WE SEE.

Visibility, accessibility, and being "in focus" are basic to being trustworthy. Absent leaders see their credibility erode over time. Trust is visceral.

WE TRUST LEADERS WE KNOW.

Except in emergencies, we're more apt to give people we know some loyalty and allegiance than we are to follow strangers.

WE TRUST SYMBOLS WE UNDERSTAND.

We fill places, titles, and events with meaning and give them symbolic power. When symbols become part of community life, it's because they make "common sense" or sense-in-the-community and are, therefore, trusted.

In Montgomery, Alabama, there's a memorial to fifty-three people who were murdered in the South during the civil rights movement of the 1950s and 1960s. Each name is inscribed in chronological order. Some of the names are familiar—Emmett Till, the four little girls who died in the bombing of the Birmingham church—while others are unknown to most of us. The memorial is made of black marble in the shape of a large circular table with a thin film of water flowing over the surface, recalling the words of the prophet, "let justice roll on like a river, / righteousness like a never-failing stream" (Am. 5:24). Maya Lin, the memorial's designer, remembers the dedication ceremony, when the participants wept. She recollects, "Emmett Till's mother was touching his name beneath the water and crying, and I realized that her tears were becoming part of the memorial."[12] It's a holy moment when a symbol takes on meaning.

WE RARELY TRUST INSTITUTIONS UNTIL THEY ARE PERSONALIZED.

Nobody seems to like big organizations, except through members of those organizations they think are helpful, friendly, and share their values. William Zinsser has it right when he notes, "...institutions and places have no life of their own. You must bring them to life with men and women and children."[13]

COACHING CONVERSATION

Does your faith community have faith in you? your accessibility? your loyalty? the symbols you represent? the face you put on your church?

Tributaries of Trust

Trust grows from several tributaries. Note the varied streams that converge to create trust:

- Trust grows from positive actions and interactions. It has a living history.
- Trust accumulates over time and tests. It builds through positive experiences.
- Trust is always fragile and precious. Trust may take years to grow and seconds to destroy.
- Trust is always deepening or dying. Trust is dynamic. It never stands still and either grows or erodes.
- Trust shows itself in our relationships with persons and groups. Trust networks itself across communities.
- Trust has a "radius," a range or reach of its impact on others. Trust builds its own momentum.

Trust is a "good experience" process with at least three primary expressions—concern, consistency, and capability.[14] These basic issues build community trust over time, if they're demonstrated over and over again. Trust is earned. So, how do leaders such as you and I behave in ways that plant, cultivate, and grow trustworthiness? Here's how I begin to trust you as my leader.

CONCERN: I TRUST YOU IF YOU SHOW ME THAT YOU CARE ABOUT ME.

I want my leaders to want the best for me. I need my leaders to believe in me. I want leaders who listen to me. I want leaders who recognize and appreciate my contributions to our community. I want leaders who encourage my heart.[15] I want leaders who love and relate to me personally. That's how concern is shown concretely.

CONSISTENCY: I TRUST YOU IF YOU PROVE TO ME THAT YOU'RE A PERSON OF INTEGRITY.

I want my leaders to help our community establish a common purpose. I want leaders who deal openly with me. I want my leaders to honor my sense of calling and my commitments. I want leaders who hold me accountable when I don't follow through on my dreams and promises. I want leaders who help our community deal with the present we have and the future God will give us. I want leaders with integrity.

Integrity is a foundation for trust. Originally, in the New Testament, integrity was a jeweler's term and meant "without wax." Dishonest jewelers disguised inferior stones by covering the flaws with wax. "Buyer beware" must have been their philosophy as they hoodwinked unsuspecting shoppers. Integrity, character, values, and credibility are shown in consistent behavior.

CAPABILITY: I TRUST YOU IF YOU HELP ME PURSUE MY CALLING IN LIFE.

I want my leaders to help our community create clear goals. I want my leaders to empower me to act. I want my leaders to calmly and steadily focus on our community's key priorities. I want my leaders to celebrate my victories with me. I want my leaders to help me face and get beyond my failures.

COACHING CONVERSATION

Leaders stay connected to their communities. When communities are divided by conflict, the issue of capability fades quickly into the background. Amid conflict, trust is proven primarily by care and character.

Recent research shows pastors of rapidly growing churches consider "pastoral ministry" their number one weakness. Ministry to individuals by means of counseling, hospital visitation, weddings, and funerals were considered "nitpicky ministry" that diverts time and energy from more important activities.[16] Avoid placing pastoral leadership and pastoral care in false tension.

Watersheds of Trust

Trust is a watershed for community. It's a mostly invisible contour of the landscape and, therefore, is frequently taken for granted until it's polluted. Trust can be lost more rapidly than it can be refurbished. Without trust, community dries up and dies.

Leaders can test their reputations for trustworthiness by checking only four test questions with their community members. Trustworthiness requires four positive answers. Consistency, clear communication, keeping promises, and being scrupulously honest are the only behaviors worthy of trust. No exceptions. Period. Leaders should ask the following:

- Do they see me behaving consistently or erratically?
- Do they see me communicating clearly or carelessly?
- Do they see me treating promises seriously or casually?
- Do they see me as honest or deceitful?

When Trust Turns to Mistrust

Trust erodes quickly when betrayed. That's the tragedy. Trust grows slowly but dies suddenly. Sometimes rumors signal the beginning of the end of trusting relationships. In general, rumors occur at the intersection of anxiety and ambiguity. When communities experience uncertain situations and unclear facts, rumors bloom. What's interesting about the rumors that buzz on community grapevines is that most are actually true. The ones that aren't factual get vastly exaggerated and become fodder for the rumor mill. Leaders learn to face rumors with a three-word mantra: *calm and clear, calm and clear, calm and clear.* In other words, they try by example to dampen anxiety and communicate the true circumstances with precision and openness.

A leadership pinch occurs when trust's threshold is crossed and generates mistrust and distrust. Then, like a seesaw, confidence and faith go down while suspicion and doubt go up. Distrust is robust and tough to mend. Amid distrust, the chances of leaders' rebuilding trust may be "slim and none." When trust is breached, leaders are in jeopardy and may have cut their umbilical to their community. If trust is irrevocably broken, leaders might as well exit, since they have lost their community connection.

Theologically, it's important to recall in Paul's teaching that reconciliation is the work of God. From a human perspective, leaders can try to manage anxiety and conflict. But if real enemies become real friends, this shows God is present. Identifying the most trusted community members and freeing them to work toward healing is one possibility amid mistrust. In the final analysis, trust will have to be given a chance to take root and grow again.

COACHING CONVERSATION

Distrust and mistrust are community killers. Rely on God's healing power and the wisdom of God's people.

The Harvest of Trust

Credibility is the harvest of trust.[17] Leaders with trustworthiness act in ways that add to their reputations:

- They ask real questions.
- They shut up and pay attention to answers.

- They listen carefully to the words, the content of others' replies, and "music"—the tone, mood, and tempo of the feedback.
- They care about the community and its members.
- They take strategic risks.
- They act with consistency.
- They give trust time to grow and mature.
- They see God at work in others and appreciate the mystery in healthy relationships.

COACHING CONVERSATION

Credibility is like gold—rare, coveted, and valuable. Work for it. Treasure it.

Families: Bays of Belief and Behavior

While friendships and trust are basins or collection points for community, our families are like bays or oceans for leaders. Our families are our theological cradles, providing continuity and collection points for what we believe and how we behave as leaders. Since congregations are gatherings of families, our families in our various forms and styles try to "commune." We combine our unique blends of health and brokenness into congregational watersheds. The overall diversity either blesses the congregational mix or fragments it.

You and I have probably learned different leadership lessons from our families of origin. All I can contribute to this discussion is some clear recognition of what I harvested about leadership from my family. Listed below you'll see some of the things I caught from my parents, my two sets of grandparents, my brothers, and an assortment of aunts, uncles, and cousins. Compare your experiences and gleanings with mine.

In the Genes

WE'RE ALL LIKE GRANDPA AND GRANDMA.

Behavior patterns—and their intensities—repeat themselves from generation to generation. The Ten Commandments say hate lives three or four generations, but love lives for thousands of generations (Ex. 20:5). That's a strong example of the staying and shaping power of our deepest emotions.

How we take initiative, face risks, and make decisions have been largely modeled by our families of origin across generations. You and I may or may not have known our forebears. It's not a matter of deliberate teaching. We carry our family's genetic code. We can't pull our roots out of the soil of earlier generations. In profound ways, we're all like parents, grandparents, and others who have given us life and genetic heritage.

WHEN YOU WERE BORN MAKES A DIFFERENCE.

Birth order influences how we lead and follow in congregational life. Firstborn leaders tend to act incrementally, think developmentally, create continuity by linking change to the past, and act in more risk-aversive ways. Later-born leaders tend to act in transformational terms, think in more revolutionary ways, create discontinuity by breaking with the past, and act in more risk-subversive ways.

WE'RE PART OF LARGER GROUPS.

You and I are part of larger wholes—families, teams, congregations, and communities. Emotional interdependency is the nature of life in communities. When anything changes in the group, everything changes in the group. A new member joins, and the community changes. An old member exits the group, and the community changes.

COACHING CONVERSATION

Families are our first communities. They teach us lessons about life and leadership when we're younger that may not sink in and be learned until we're older.

Families and Communities Pool Their Anxiety

Living beings carry anxiety around inside them. Leaders learn to recognize and regulate their anxiety.

TRIANGULAR RELATIONSHIPS ARE EVERYWHERE AND FOREVER.

We relate in triangular configurations. The "odd man out" form takes the edge off anxiety. In fact, the triangle is the shape of mother-in-law jokes. Since we can't avoid triangles, we learn to recognize them, observe them, and stay out of the indirect, stressful position in them.

ANXIETY IS CONTAGIOUS.

We all catch and pass along anxiety. The fear of what may be is contagious. Leaders may damp down anxiety, acting as circuit breakers. Or we may ramp up anxiety, acting as transformers to generate more uncertainty. Since frightened communities turn on themselves, wise leaders serve as circuit breakers or immune systems by multiplying calm and enhancing group health.

IT'S EASIER TO GET SCARED THAN TO STAY CALM.

Living persons get anxious and scared. It's the nature of all living protoplasm. Three powerful anxiety binders—relationships, beliefs, and success—are especially spooky to us. Leaders, therefore, work on staying calm, centered, clear, and concise.

COACHING CONVERSATION

There are no "anxiety-free zones" for leaders. But we can—and must—learn to recognize anxious patterns, monitor and regulate our responses, and concentrate on staying centered.

Leaders Are Home-Grown

You've taken on an important function—leader. An early challenge is to get connected to your community. Then a few other leader challenges are always in front of you.

INSIDES ARE MORE IMPORTANT THAN OUTSIDES.

Defining who we are is an "inside out" process and takes our entire life span to achieve. Growing our belief system and keeping our integrity is an endless challenge. As leaders, we hope our values and our community's values finally flow together. But, even if this melding doesn't happen, don't lose self and your core beliefs.

DON'T EXPECT APPLAUSE.

Challenges to the status quo are usually met with resistance in the forms of sabotage or seduction. For those of us who need to be liked, conflict is especially painful. In the face of rebellion in the ranks, we've been taught to think industrially—analyze, diagnose, identify symptoms, study demographics, and review content. Generally, we'd be better off to look at process and context. Amid conflict, get out of your head and trust your heart. Nurture your connections to your community. Keep yourself centered. Monitor and regulate your reactions. Stay steady. And, don't get addicted to applause, because the audience may be quiet, or, at the very least, not affirming.

IN THE END, DRAMATIC CHANGE IS RARE.

Congregations and other communities prefer to stay in balance. Becoming healthier is the primary way leaders and communities may really change. Leaders work from their connections if they intend to challenge what has been. At the same time, leaders stand on the edge of their communities and point to options. Outsiders may break communities, but they rarely change them.

LEADERS WEAR THE BELL.

You may have heard the term *bellwether*. Domesticated animals organize themselves naturally so that one sheep or cow or goat takes the lead in the herd. Herdsmen and farmers know they can find their animals easily by taking one simple action—they put a bell on the leader. When herdsmen hear the bell, they've found the entire herd.

Leaders wear the bell. To heighten immunity, community leaders learn where they begin and end, grow their beliefs and goals, focus on staying centered and calm, and keep their connections to their groups current and strong. When leaders speak with clear "I messages," they convey their core, their boundaries, and their hopes without disrespecting others in the community.

COACHING CONVERSATION

Leaders are lifelong learners. They begin as children to absorb some lessons by osmosis. As adults, they function more like archeologists to unearth and decode the bones and flesh of their lives. Yet, they rarely get completely beyond the reach of their cradles. How they respond amid sunshine or storm is often shaped by what they've learned on their journey toward selfhood and leadership. Their responses are often watersheds for the congregation and for themselves.

Leadership Watersheds

Watersheds serve two obvious functions in creation. First, they divide water and differentiate one basin's flow pattern from others. Second, they pool water and direct it forward into a common channel. Likewise, faith communities serve the same two basic human needs:

They help to define who's in and who's out, who's near and who's far, as well as to bring persons with mutuality together. Without community, there are no leaders. That's a watershed. Without leaders, there are no long-term communities. That, too, is a watershed.

✔ CASE STUDY: Matt's Web of Relationships

Matt has always had a knack for being likable. He always considered himself a friendly guy. As a firstborn, he worked at being responsible, intelligent, and accessible. His special training in the behavioral sciences helped him understand communities. Like most of us, Matt's parents, wife, and children were built-in laboratories for learning more about creating friendships and trust. A school experience with one of his children opened the door for a first exposure to family systems. Later, with more formal study of Bowen theory, Matt gained an entirely new understanding of how relationships form and then ebb and flow. He became a more deliberate connector—and an even more effective connector—with people. Matt learned to see and deal with triangles.

Growing Immune Communities

Immunizing the body of Christ is an essential function of connected congregational leadership. Immunity is about who we are, not what we do. In organic terms, immunity deals with the health of living communities. Immunity reveals the core of our community, identifying the "me" and distinguishing it from the "not-me." Congregational DNA flows from shared history, common belief, and defining decisions. DNA shows who we are, what we stand for, and our place in the larger family of faith.

Immunity in the human body isn't lodged in any single organ. Rather, it's body-wide. Our entire body is involved in preserving its own health. Enhancing the "me" and resisting the "not-me" is a multiplied function with skin barriers, stomach acids, and white cells at the ready. Congregational immunity systems call on clusters of leaders who understand the heart and soul of their unique faith community. Like Martin Luther, the immune system of any community affirms, "Here I stand." Immunity for communities is a web of connections.

Connecting: Job One

Connections create community. Friends, trust, and family relationships flow together in the watershed communities we call

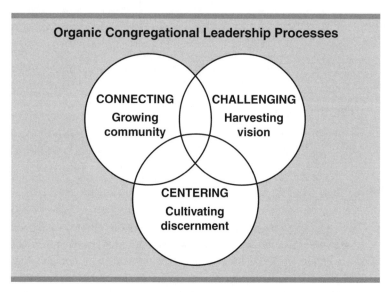

Organic Congregational Leadership Processes

CONNECTING
Growing
community

CHALLENGING
Harvesting
vision

CENTERING
Cultivating
discernment

congregations. Now, let's review our model for organic leadership and explore centering and challenging our community next.

James Burke, the host of the British Broadcasting Corporation's *Connections* series about how one innovation links to another, notes change occurs in "the way things come together and connect."[18] Connected communities, once formed, look for centers and challenges. They are our next destinations in exploring leadership as organic processes.

CHAPTER 5

Centering 101

Growing Community Depth

What kinds of communities do you belong to? How many communities are you part of? What kind of communities do you try to grow and lead?

Sociologists identify two kinds of communities: bounded and centered. Bounded communities set up clear perimeters and defend their boundaries. They concentrate on keeping "bad folks" out and "good folks" in. Bounded communities are defined by limits—what they're against—and "weeding." In contrast, centered communities revolve around clear purposes, core callings, and central needs. They are defined by love, folks drawn into the community, and "seeding." In the organic leadership process in this book, we're more focused on centered and centering communities. The reason is simple.

Centered communities have depth. We'll examine what lies below the surface of centered communities.

The Tip of the Iceberg

We've often heard the expression, "The tip of the iceberg." That's because only about 1/8 of the mass of an iceberg is visible above water. Icebergs, literally "ice mountains" in the Dutch language, form when glaciers or polar ice sheets break on their seaward sides. Glaciers form on land, the net accumulation of snow over thousands of years. Their sheer weight causes them to creep or flow downhill. When glaciers reach the ocean, pieces break off and become icebergs. There they sink into the salt water and move around the ocean, pure water surrounded by briny sea.

LEADER'S LEXICON

"Iceberg," an ice mountain floating in the sea, and, in this case, a metaphor for the largely hidden spiritual centers for leadership.

The small part of icebergs that is visible uses the invisible parts as ballast, weight to provide stability to or to steady the massive bulk of ice. The invisible 7/8 of the iceberg centers the visible 1/8. That's exactly what a spiritual center lends to a faith community. It steadies and gives stability in an otherwise turbulent sea.

Approaches to Help Us Center Ourselves

What gives ballast and balance to leaders? What centers us? What gives us a sense of self and a heart for others? Let's look at six discovery approaches that can help us center ourselves for leadership:

- The actions Jesus took to find center for himself and give center to others,
- Our strengths for leadership
- Life's stage-by-stage lessons
- A center-growing model
- A community discernment process
- The fruit of the Spirit

Leaders and communities are defined by centers. The challenge is to find, deliberately claim, and make those centers more overt for ourselves and to our faith communities.

Jesus: Finding Center

Jesus centered himself. He anchored and stimulated his own growth primarily through his relationship to his Father and by several other secondary channels. He spoke eloquently of his summary beliefs: "'Love the Lord your God with all your heart and with all your soul and with all your mind.' This is the first and greatest commandment. And the second is like it: 'Love your neighbor as

yourself.' All the Law and the Prophets hang on these two commandments" (Mt. 22:37–40).

Read the list below with the life of Christ in mind and attach
biblical incidents and passages of Scripture to each of them as you
consider how Jesus centered himself:

• Seeking out good mentors and teachers
• Immersing his mind and soul in Scripture
• Worshiping and praying as a regular pattern
• Clarifying his calling
• Risking his ideas and calling in the marketplace
• Sharpening his identity over time
• Wrestling with God's will
• Submitting his will to God
• Giving his life for others

Which Bible stories or references came to mind as you thought about
the ways Jesus centered himself?

On the other hand, Jesus pointed others to their centers in a rich
variety of ways:

• Answering questions
• Asking questions
• Allowing others to shadow and observe him
• Permitting failure and giving second chances
• Telling stories with many links listeners could identify with
• Pointing strugglers to the foundations of Scripture
• Letting some persons turn away
• Forcing others to confront bias and blind spots
• Challenging the future with vision

Did Bible incidents flash through your memory and imagination as
you considered how Jesus helped others deepen their lives?

COACHING CONVERSATION

As with the submerged portions of icebergs, we may not see more than 1/8
of Jesus' centering approaches. He used multiple paths to center. Jesus
rooted himself in the middle, but he planted his ministries on the margins.

Cultivating Our Built-in Centers

The Gallup organization is known for its polling services, particularly on political issues. However, they also do high-quality leader development. Their formula sounds like an emphasis on spiritual gifts. Gallup encourages leaders to become stewards of strengths.[1] They suggest spending 90 percent of our time stewarding our strengths and only 10 percent of our effort on managing our weaknesses.

The idea is simple. God has already planted gifts for leadership and ministry in us. We have only to focus on and use these gifts well. The array of strengths God has blessed us with is impressive: our spiritual gifts, those things we do well, what satisfies and rewards us, what we know the most about, our natural abilities, and whatever is second-nature to us. Each of these strengths is a discovery channel for our spiritual center as leaders.

OUR DISCOVERY CHANNELS

Would you like to become clearer about your strengths? There are five "discovery channels" for this find-and-use process. One key to these discoveries is to listen attentively to our self-talk, our internal conversations. What do you "say to yourself" at life's turning points? These are often life's learning points as well.

1. **Transcending**—those times in our days when life goes on "automatic" and we say:

   "I was 'in the zone.'"
   "Time stopped."
   "I didn't miss a beat."
   "I was 'at one' with that."

2. **Excelling**—those moments of true excellence we experience and we say:

   "I do this really well."
   "I'm a natural at this."
   "This is a 'no sweat' activity."
   "Why can't everyone do this easily too?"
   "I see how to do this without effort."

3. **Learning**—those times in life when we're "quick studies" and we say:

"I 'get' this."
"This is simple."
"This is easy for me."
"Why would anyone have trouble with this?"
"I feel like I've always known this."

4. **Rewarding**–noting those occasions in life when we feel particularly satisfied and we say:

"What fun!"
"This feels great."
"I get a kick out of that."
"I can hardly wait to do that again...and again."

5. **Attracting**–identifying life's magnets, those experiences that call out to our hearts and we say:

"I love doing that."
"I'd like to try that."
"I know I can do that."
"That looks like great fun."
"That seems so interesting to me."

Take a moment and review your own discovery channels. When have you realized that you have a gift for leadership by listening to your self-talk?

COACHING CONVERSATION

When Jesus reminded us that our hearts and our treasures mirror each other (Mt. 6:21), he was giving us a wonderful way to discover the gifts he has embedded in us. Watch your discovery channels. Use your strengths well.

Lifelong Leader Lessons

Leadership is a lifelong learning process. It challenges us at every stage of life. "Center" for leaders calls them to learn several central lessons and to wrestle with basic questions as life's seasons visit and revisit them. The questions below focus and refocus leaders as they grow and unfold across their life spans.[2] Find the questions that fit your life stage and answer them. Then, get ready for the next flurry of questions a new life stage will bring to you. Answering each of these questions is an act of faith.

- **Apprentice leaders learn to answer:**
  - How will I shape a life dream and give it a structure?
  - How will I form mentor relationships?
  - How will I find and mold a calling?
  - How will I grow loving relationships with friends and family?

- **Young leaders learn to answer:**
  - How can I root my life in relationships, calling, and community?
  - How can I discover my unique "voice" and become my own person?

  Many observers see midlife as a watershed. Bob Buford describes age forty-five as "halftime,"[3] the life stage in which we shift our attention from success to significance. Buford takes this new life focus of significance so seriously that he calls it "Life II,"[4] an era with new questions and new challenges.

- **Mid-life leaders learn to answer:**
  - How will I look back in order to look ahead?
  - How can I test new choices?
  - Which old doors will I close, and which new ones will I open?

- **Mature leaders learn to answer:**
  - Who am I finally?
  - Where do I belong?
  - What do I care about?
  - What is my legacy?

Review your life's progress to date. How have you dealt with the questions that have bubbled up in your ministry?

COACHING CONVERSATION

The good news is that life keeps on bringing us fresh questions. The bad news is life keeps on bringing us fresh questions. Like onions, life and leadership provide us with new layers to explore. Sometimes life's "onions" bring us a few tears too.

Seeds for the Future

✔ CASE STUDY: Matt's Life Review

As Matt neared retirement, he intentionally stepped back and took inventory. Where was he in the end-of-active-ministry process? And, where was his church? He adopted a deliberate approach toward coaching key leaders to anticipate his retirement transition. Matt helped them think through the issues the church would likely face when he retired. He talked about his retirement plans with the congregation's leadership team. He timed his announcements to the larger congregation to keep the anxiety down as much as he could. His questions helped him frame and face a major ministry transition.

Modeling Centering Growth

Leaders want to tap the 7/8 of life that's hidden below the surface. The model below suggests growth in two less-than-obvious directions— our best selves in God and our congregation's best sense of God's will.

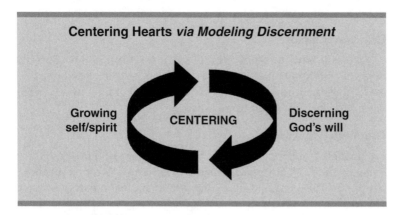

Growing Center for Leaders: Identity

Like congregations, leaders' souls are alive, too. And, like all living things, leaders' souls are dynamic—flowering or fading, expanding or shriveling. It's as easy to overlook the importance of soul growth as it is to ignore the 7/8 of icebergs that "live" beneath the surfaces of our oceans. After all, congregational leaders invest huge amounts of their energy into the souls of others.

Still, we must remember that *our* souls are the ballast, the anchors, and the root systems for *our* functioning as leaders. Our souls steady and "right" us; they orient us toward meaning in our lives. In fact, "soul" is more than the eternal aspect of our beings. Soul includes everything that you know really matters in your life. Whatever draws us closer to God, whatever helps us open our lives to God in deeper places, that's what grows souls. Jesus reminded us of our spiritual dependence on him, "I am the vine; you are the branches. If a man remains in me and I in him, he will bear much fruit; apart from me you can do nothing" (Jn. 15:5). To neglect our souls is to invite burnout, discouragement, and ineffectiveness.

A variety of spiritual exercises strengthen our souls and center us in Christ:

CENTERING BOOKS

For those of us who were raised on Scripture, we recognize the Bible is the paramount centering book. It provides the touchstone, a foundation to which we return daily. Which books of the Bible, and books *other* than the Bible, do we read over and over again? Note them, and lean on them. Intuitively, we know these materials grow our souls, and we revisit them for nourishment. Varying from person to person, they bring us "home" to our core beliefs and best self.

CENTERING FRIENDS

Do you have a friend who tells you the truth about yourself? Persons who know us, still love us, and can hold mirrors before us are centering forces in our lives. Soul friends don't get in our space except to lift us up when we're down.

CENTERING FAILURES

Trouble is a telling trigger in life. Failures make our souls either thrive or shrivel. They make us better or leave us more anxious about our abilities and future. In the Old Testament, Jacob had to face his lifelong pattern of taking ethical shortcuts. At the Jabbok ford, he wrestled with God through the night, injuring his hip. From that day forward, his limp reminded him about his life's failures and centers. Some have described that the families of persons who died in Nazi concentration camps feel "a presence of an absence." What a poetic way to identify the centering impact of trouble and loss on our lives!

CENTERING PRAYERS

We all need open, surrendered, peaceful ways of resting in God's presence. The psalmist speaks of the stilled and quieted soul (Ps. 131:2). Cultivate the regular practice of centering or contemplative prayer. Open your life to God.

Centering Solitudes

We live in a crowded world. Moments of solitude are precious. The sixteenth-century mystic Saint John of the Cross claimed silence was God's first language. Interior silence and a quiet heart can help us find and anchor ourselves. Listen to your feelings and to your wishes. Beginning with an ear to our inner voices is a first step to hearing God's voice within us.

Centering Simplicities

A new profession has grown up around helping people manage clutter in their homes and lives. We can easily make our personal and professional worlds complicated. But complexity is less the enemy of the soul than duplicity. Jesus challenged his followers to be single-minded: "No one can serve two masters. Either he will hate the one and love the other, or he will be devoted to the one and despise the other" (Mt. 6:24).

Centering Weaknesses

None of us is happy to be weak. And, our weaknesses, if unrecognized and unfaced, can crush us. In his classic treatment on Christian ethics, L. H. Marshall unmasks the "hypocrites" of the Gospels. Rather than perceiving these persons as acting or playing a part, Marshall sees the hypocrites as having moral blind spots. Marshall noted, "They were so blinded by self-complacency, spiritual pride, and self-conceit that they could see no wrong in themselves...".[5] As leaders, we particularly need to know and guard against our weaknesses, or our blind spots will cut us off from our communities.

We rightly rely on our strengths and spiritual gifts as leaders. But occasionally we need the chastening reminder that we don't live by strength alone. For instance, in a former pastorate, I had a key church member who was a thorn in my flesh. Nothing I did was good enough or religious enough or visionary enough to suit her. At one point she began a systematic house-to-house visitation to announce I was a dangerous radical of some sort. Although her conclusion was untrue and her actions were misguided, several member families were hurt and drew back from me. While I was trying to reconnect with these wounded families, I reached out to her, too. She wanted nothing to do with me, although she remained actively involved in our church. Then, I had a fateful conversation with her husband one evening. The two of us were alone in the church building. I risked an admission of weakness to him. Calling her by name, I said, "I don't know how to be her pastor. What can I do?" His eyes filled with tears, and he replied, "I don't know. I've been married to her for thirty years, and I don't even know how to be her husband!" A bond formed between us at that moment that lasted until his death. And, my connection with her husband kept her within the radius of my pastoral outreach. It was a "soul moment" and a key learning experience for me in pastoral "leadercraft." I learned that, although we use our strengths as stewardship, we can minister and lead from weakness as well.

B. B. King, the blues musician whose guitar is named Lucille, answered an interviewer's question wisely. To the inquiry about whether or not during hard times he'd ever considered pawning Lucille, King replied: "You can't play the blues until you've been pawned!" Weakness contains the seeds of opportunity.

COACHING CONVERSATION

Deepen your strengths. It isn't selfish to invest in yourself. Grow the garden of your soul every way you can. Cultivating your best self is the best way to become a better leader.

Growing Centered Communities: Discernment

Faith communities find their center in God's will. From the Greek for "to sift through," *discernment* is usually discovered by praying and seeking God, listening to God and people of faith in our communities, opening our imaginations to fresh options and to the surprises of God, and taking time to let God's clarity emerge in our communities. Discernment is an act of faith, our dawning discovery that makes us "certain of what we do not see" (Heb. 11:1). Discernment is listening to God and to each other rather than telling each other what to do or merely voting against each other.

Discernment is timely in our era of information and experience, partly because it may stretch the root systems of our own faith backgrounds. For example, my Baptist polity emerges primarily from the English parliamentary and American town meeting heritages. When Baptist congregations make decisions, the majority rules. Although we may say we're seeking God's will for our congregation, we sometimes just settle for the side that can muster the most votes. Likewise, your denomination's ways of making decisions likely grow out of the historical era in which your group began and the patterns of government of that culture. These practices may or may not work well in our era.

We arrived at this juncture in congregational decision-making by an interesting route. A Baptist and an army officer, Henry Martyn Robert, was asked to help a congregation face a decision with the potential for lots of conflict. In true military fashion, he drafted some rules of engagement, a set of principles for warfare. Robert's rules worked fairly well, and his reputation as a mediator grew. Soon others were asking for his rules. The manual, *Robert's Rules of Order*, was the result. Parliamentarians for churches and other deliberative bodies were born. Decisions now had rules for debate, disagreement, and decision-making. Structures were provided to deliberative bodies to clarify, slow, and manage large-scale and contentious decisions.[6]

DISCERNING GOD'S WILL FOR INDIVIDUALS: A BEGINNING POINT

Some Christians are now wearying of such dependence on parliamentary rules. Drawing on older patterns of faith—especially the monastic and mystical traditions—they are calling for "discern-mentarians." If you or your congregation adopted a discernmentarian style of decision making, what would you do and how would you act?

Actually, discernment as a spiritual practice has both an individual and a congregational expression. The Quaker tradition has used "clearness committees" for individual discernment.[7] For example, if I had an issue I wanted to pursue until I was assured of God's will, I could invite a cluster of persons to join me in a discernment process. I'd tell them the issue I was unclear about, invite their questions and prayers, and wait—perhaps over multiple sessions—until I was finally clear about the matter. Then, I'd share my conviction with my group, thank them, and dissolve this clearness committee. That's an individual journey toward discernment.

COACHING CONVERSATION

Leaders help their communities find direction and move ahead with clarity. They demonstrate that there are focusing issues of belief and spirit that are more edifying than just a matter of who can muster the most votes or generate the greatest political leverage.

DISCERNING GOD'S WILL FOR CONGREGATIONS: THE LARGER ISSUE

Discernment also has a community-wide dimension. How can your faith community actively and corporately search for God's will for its present and future? Is there an organic discernment approach for clarifying the will of God for a congregation's life?

An organic model for discerning God's will guides a congregational process clearly:

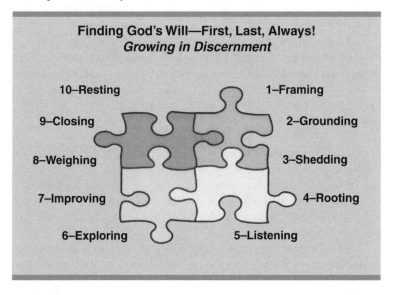

Finding God's Will—First, Last, Always!
Growing in Discernment

10–Resting
9–Closing
8–Weighing
7–Improving
6–Exploring

1–Framing
2–Grounding
3–Shedding
4–Rooting
5–Listening

CHOOSING DISCERNMENT'S SEEDS

• Framing Discernment–Discernment calls for a clearly stated issue, a "mental model," or an arena for exploration. Framing questions for congregations include: Are we clear about the specific issue for discernment? Is this really a discernment matter for our congregation? God, what are you guiding us toward?

COACHING CONVERSATION

Spotlight centering issues. Get extremely clear about what you're asking God to reveal. Seeds are important. The Scripture is wise when it reminds us, "A man reaps what he sows" (Gal. 6:7b). Remember how often Jesus talked about God's kingdom? It was his mental model of ministry.

PLANTING DISCERNMENT'S SEEDS

• Grounding Discernment–Discernment roots itself within a boundary or around a guiding principle. I like the grounding principle Morris and Olsen apply: the will of God–nothing more, nothing less, nothing else.[8] Grounding questions might involve: Is the kingdom of God our ideal? Is this our Gethsemane struggle to find and do God's will?

- Shedding for Discernment—Discernment challenges us to lay aside anything that keeps us from focusing on God's will as our ultimate value. Some questions about shedding might ask: What needs to die in us for God to have room to direct our lives? What must we release for God to begin something new? Where and why are we broken before the Lord?

- Rooting for Discernment—Discernment emerges from a root system and a foundation. A variety of rooting questions offer strength. What passage of Scripture or which hymn gives us a place to stand? What person, parable, story, or image provides an anchor for discernment here? What theme from theology, church history, art, or literature lends a metaphor for discernment?

COACHING CONVERSATION

Now the discernment process is underway. Time spent in preparation for congregational quests for the will of God is time well spent. The seedbed makes the difference in whether good seeds have a chance to root and produce. Jesus spent forty days in the wilderness as he explored the shape his ministry would take (Mt. 4:1–11; Lk. 4:1–13). Paul's radical conversion sent him away to discern the contours of his new life as well. What are our boundaries? What has to go? Where can we stand?

CULTIVATING DISCERNMENT'S PLANTINGS

- Listening for Discernment—Discernment calls for "ears to hear" the illuminating voices of God and his communities. Listening questions tune our ears and hearts to a myriad of voices. What is God's Spirit saying to us? Whose unheard voices do we need to listen for? Whose personal pain or perspectives can sensitize us? Whose intuitions and needs can alert us to God-at-work in us?

  Have you noticed how often churches talk bravely about reaching out to a new people group—without any direct contact with the group? Some churches are using focus groups to help them understand the needs of special audiences in their communities.

- Exploring for Discernment—Discernment emerges out of many options. Exploration questions include: Can we identify at least four alternative solutions? Where is God trying to surprise, challenge, or stretch us in this discernment process?

• Improving for Discernment–Discernment expects to discover God's will in the best (not just the good) and in the most (not the least). Questions designed to improve the quality of the process involve: How can we "better up" our options? How can we make each alternative the best it can be? How can we avoid the lowest common denominator?

COACHING CONVERSATION

Discernment may become hands-on leadership at this stage. To use an organic gardening example, most of the new "designer" fruits and vegetables are hand-pollinated.[9] Discernment, like horticulture and midwifery, looks for healthy outcomes—and that usually requires "face time."

REAPING DISCERNMENT'S HARVEST

• Weighing Possibilities–Discernment calls for discrimination and wise judgment. Questions that aid the weighing process include: On which option does the Spirit rest? How can we "test the spirits" (1 Jn. 4:1) and find wisdom? Can we wait patiently until the Spirit rests? Which fruits of the Spirit would our alternatives produce?

• Closing on Our Decision–Discernment produces a decision and closure. Some questions to draw our decision-making to a close include: How can we test for consensus and accord? Have we prayed, listened, and waited long enough? Are we practicing our guiding principle? If still undecided, are we willing to let our most spiritually mature member decide for us? Choosing Book-of-the-Month selections was a discernment process. A panel of five judges made the decision. Three of the five had Quaker backgrounds and persuaded the group to use the Quaker method of concurrence. Any potential book that gained the concurrence of the entire group was selected.[10] Otherwise, that book was dropped from consideration. There was a sense that the books chose themselves.

• Resting in Our Decision–Discernment, if we have found God's will, reassures us. With time, some questions attest to the wisdom of our discernment process. Is this a comfortable and untroubled decision? Has it brought consolation, peace, and joy? Has it brought desolation, heaviness, and a troubled spirit? Has this decision moved me and us toward God? Patrick Henry was clear and crisp in his challenge to the gathering at Richmond's St. John's Church in Virginia's Provincial Convention in 1775, "Give me liberty or give me death." There's no evidence the first draft of his speech said, "Give me ambiguity or maybe give me something else." Centering brings clarity to our message.

COACHING CONVERSATION

The proof of the pudding is in the eating. Discernment actually begins the larger leadership challenge—finding our futures and harvesting the fruit of our ministries.

Fruit of the Spirit

Jesus said the proof of a prophetic spirit is fruit we produce (Mt. 7:16). Paul extends and comments on the organic image of "the fruit of the Spirit" (Gal. 5:22–23). Paul's list is daunting for Christian leaders, especially in sharp contrast with the evil acts mentioned earlier in the passage (Gal. 5:19–21). These evil acts are community-breakers, setting us selfishly against God and our faith families.

In stark distinction to these evil acts, the fruits of love, joy, peace, patience, kindness, goodness, faithfulness, gentleness, and self-control are community-makers.[11] They bless relationships and provide proof of leaders' fitness to set the pace in faith communities. The fruit of the Spirit strengthen all kinds of relationships, but, in the context of faith, they are magnified.

All of the Spirit's fruits are important, but a few of these fruits of the Spirit are noted below as particularly crucial to organic leaders.

ORGANIC LEADERS KNOW PEACE IS GOD'S HARVEST.

In the New Testament, the word *peace* often had a civic or community meaning. It spoke of the serenity a people enjoyed under a good leader. Or it referred to a person who was charged with keeping the peace in a community. Here it probably describes the tranquility of resting our lives in God's grip.

ORGANIC LEADERS CULTIVATE PATIENCE WITH PEOPLE.

Patience pointed to leaders who had the power to avenge wrongs but chose to forgive, forbear, forget, and to use wholesome restraint. Organic leaders can afford to cultivate patience. They are part of their communities for the long haul, in contrast to mechanistic leaders who may concentrate on the short run.

ORGANIC LEADERS PRODUCE RELIABILITY.

Faithfulness, or trustworthiness, forms a base for leaders. Credibility can be grown or forfeited.[12] Reliability grows from trustworthiness, confidence, and faith.

ORGANIC LEADERS GROW SELF-MASTERY.

Self-control speaks of regulating our responses and facing our overreactions. It describes an athlete's discipline (1 Cor. 9:25), a believer's exercise of self-denial (1 Cor. 7:9), and the ruler's virtue in not placing self-interest over the needs of the governed. At its best, self-mastery means leaders have such control over their own lives that they are fit to serve others wisely and well. This self-regulation happens largely beneath the surface.

✔ **CASE STUDY: Matt Plumbs the Depths**

Matt's spiritual growth was typical of many persons in his denomination and era in history. He was a student of Scripture and practiced prayer as a basic discipline. Then, systems thinking reframed his view of Scripture, linking the overall movement of God in the world more clearly. However, the big difference for Matt emerged when he traveled back to his family's original homeland of Wales, where he discovered the richness of Celtic Christianity. The Celtic approach to community life and to evangelism stretched and deepened Matt's faith as well as his leadership practices.

Look beneath the Ocean's Surface

Icebergs are impressive—and would be awe-inspiring if only we could see their full dimensions. What lessons are there for leaders about centering processes "under the surface"?

CENTERS ARE POWERFUL BUT NOT ALWAYS OBVIOUS.

As has already been mentioned, icebergs are mostly under the surface of water and are, therefore, deceptive in size. Centering, although absolutely critical to faith communities and their leaders, hides a lot of the power of their invisible, spiritual centers. Like an iceberg, the "size" of a spiritual center is deceptive. That lack of "mass" may cause outsiders to underestimate the heft of a spiritual center and move against the community with boldness. Conversely, it may invite insiders to underutilize the resource of that center and wade in the shallows.

CENTERS ARE SOURCES OF REPLENISHMENT.

Icebergs are floating masses of pure, freshwater ice and have potential for providing drinking water. Icebergs vary in size, but they can be massive. The largest observed iceberg was estimated to have weighed more than nine billion tons, containing enough fresh water to supply every human on earth with a liter of water every day for more than four years. In the Atlantic off the coast of Newfoundland, the average iceberg weighs more than ten million tons and is roughly the size of a fifteen-story building, if that structure were cubed.

CENTERS MAY MULTIPLY.

Icebergs "calve" or fracture into separate pieces and finally melt. Larger pieces are still referred to as icebergs, but smaller ones are called "growlers." Similarly, spiritual centers multiply. They are contagious and spread their impact. The New Testament described the reach of spiritual centers sometimes in images of yeast and sometimes in pictures of salt and light (Mt. 5:13–16).

Centered Immunity

Centering a faith community in the will of God tells outsiders what to expect from the group. It's apparent this community relies on God as leader. It's also obvious that this community believes God is active among his people, guiding and shaping them. Those me-versus-not-me questions are easier to answer. The center is identified by the common discernment of God's will. We know who we are, what we believe, and to whom we belong. Our leaders know this clarity gives tremendous stability and strength, like the 7/8 of the iceberg's bulk that's below our sight lines.

Discerning how to respond to good-bad, right-wrong, or just-unjust decisions is usually fairly obvious. As faith communities, we try to choose the good, right, and just directions. God's will is straightforward in those cases. The tougher discernment challenge emerges, however, when we are forced to decide between two goods, two rights, or two conditions of justice. That's when we search for, to quote the great American jurist Oliver Wendell Holmes, "the simplicity on the other side of complexity."[13] Who am I? What's my spiritual and moral center? How can I separate the important from the urgent? How can I create a quiet space in my life to discern God's call? These simplifying questions[14] give focus to leaders and to their faith communities.

Back to Basics

Centering is one of three basic leadership processes. We've explored two of the three with one more to go. Review the model below before we move ahead.

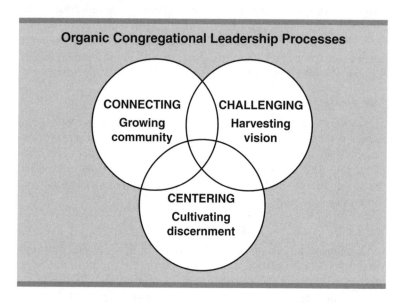

Organic Congregational Leadership Processes

CONNECTING
Growing community

CHALLENGING
Harvesting vision

CENTERING
Cultivating discernment

Now let's move on to the ways leaders practice the "challenging" process.

CHAPTER 6

Challenging 101

Growing Community Height

Vision. That's the generic answer for what leaders need most. In the majority of leadership literature, vision is job one, the first and most frequent quality that's listed. We want our leaders to have a sense of direction. That's a given. But, it's also a narrow view of what moves communities forward. Admittedly, I practiced, wrote, and taught the vision-based approach for a long time. But I've tempered that way of thinking somewhat now. And, there's a good explanation for my change of mind.

Over the years I've noticed that many leaders and faith communities knew exactly what to do—but still did not pursue their vision. They had no failure of vision. They had a failure of nerve.[1] Leaders, especially in this era of blur and uncertainty, need both courage and vision. There is no comfort in life's stretch zones, and no stretch in our comfort zones.

Without courage, vision is dead on arrival. Too often we are double-minded about change. We want life to remain the same—but get better. That natural schizophrenia raises questions. How can we lead when we feel torn about moving ahead? What provides future-oriented centers of power and energy for leaders? What grows courage in the hearts of leaders and faith communities? How do we "in-courage" ourselves as leaders and as faith communities to envision and pursue God's future? How can we find light and health?

LEADER'S LEXICON

"Courage," the capacity for taking spiritual risks and the need for leaders to be "in-couraged," drawing on the strength of inner clarity and vision.

Facing the Sun

Some plants are aggressive "sun seekers." Called "heliotropic"– from "sun" plus "turn"–these plants use sunlight as their orienting stimulus and have the ability to turn their leaves toward the sun's direct rays. Heliotropes track the sun. Most legumes and many desert annuals show heliotropic movements.

LEADER'S LEXICON

"Heliotropes," plants that follow the sun's arc, and, in this case, a metaphor for the way leaders face and draw strength from their power source.

Sunflowers are the best-known heliotropes. The operative word here is *sun.* For sunflowers, the more sun they can soak up the better. Sunflowers seem to anticipate the dawn, follow the sun's path all day long, and dread the sunset. They get full radiation to stimulate photosynthesis and maximum growth. It's a strong image for leaders, isn't it? To constantly face their source of power and inspiration is a key to growth and change. Like sunflowers, leaders are sun-chasers. They recognize clearly where their light comes from.

Laurie Beth Jones tells of taking art lessons and getting wise advice from her teacher about light sources: "'Before you begin any drawing, you must first identify your source of light…Knowing where the light is coming from will affect every aspect of your drawing. Such items as shading, depth, and volume are affected in major ways by the light source. Learn to identify it before you even begin to sketch. If you leave your drawing and then come back to it later, remember that in order to keep it consistent you must have the same source of light.'"[2] Leaders learn quickly to find and face their power source. They are drawn toward their life-giving power source. As leaders, we need to challenge persons and communities to move toward their source of light.

The Reality of Challenging Communities

How can we challenge our communities to find and follow their power source? Max DePree has famously described the beginning challenge for leaders: "The first responsibility of a leader is to define reality."[3] Leaders, acting as immune systems, take stands. They advocate for the kingdom of God. They challenge communities to become healthier and to take risks. They confront the status quo and attract persons to new projects.[4] They make a case for the future without putting others on trial. They find a place to stand and stands to take. They face the sun, or, in theological terms, they face the *Son.*

Let's explore three rich elements of challenge:

1. Courage to challenge ourselves and our communities
2. Vision to stretch ourselves and our communities
3. Nerve to stand for intentional revolutions

All these issues point us toward our source of light and power.

Seizing our best futures presses us to grow courage and harvest vision. In the model noted below, leaders use vision as gravity, lodestar, purpose, and mission. This vision is given visibility, muscle, and nerve by leaders' courage. Organic communities are heliotropic, following their power source.

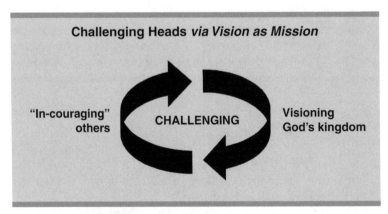

Challenging Heads *via Vision as Mission*

"In-couraging" others   CHALLENGING   Visioning God's kingdom

Growing Challenging Leaders: Courage

Courage is heart. In fact, *coeur* is the French word for "heart." Interestingly, looking at our strong emotions is a basic way to map arenas for our courage, for heart.

- Anxiety, whatever unsettles or unnerves us, invites courage to anchor us.

- Fear, whatever awakes a sense of danger or dread in us, calls for a courageous response from us.

- Anger, whatever enrages or at least creates inner storms in us, opens the door to the courage to face ourselves calmly.

- Surprises, whatever takes us unawares and signals events or discoveries we didn't expect, jolts us toward new arenas for courage.

- Resolve, whatever moves us to action, gives focus to our courage.

Courage, or following our hearts, comes from our energy source or sun, nourishing and sustaining us. Courage gives us the ability to last. In the words of the Norwegian proverb, "Heroism consists of hanging on one minute longer."

Courage isn't the absence of fear. Courage faces fear and takes risks. As one mother correctly advised her child, "You can't be brave unless you're scared." Harper Lee, author of the classic novel *To Kill a Mockingbird,* once described the courage of the Atticus Finch character in her book in almost theological terms, "Real courage is when you know you're licked before you begin, but you begin anyway."[5]

COACHING CONVERSATION

Theologically speaking, courage's equation is the sum of faith added to hope (C=F+H). Believing that God already holds our lives in his hands and hoping that God will shape all our futures by his hand, we have courage to lead.

MODELING COURAGE: FIVE ELEMENTS

What are the ingredients of courage? Although we lead in ill-defined and perilous times, the base of courage is always reflected in the leader's heart. The first Westerner to scale Mount Everest, the mountaineer Sir Edmund Hillary, wisely observed, "It's not the mountain we conquer, but ourselves."

One practical model depicts five action elements in courage for leaders.[6] These five factors blend into a mosaic of courage and map the terrain for us. Stating the model in simple terms, courage is a mosaic of candor, purpose, will, rigor, and risk.

1. *Candor:* Courage for speaking and hearing truth.
2. *Purpose:* Courage for making the sky the limit.
3. *Will:* Courage for can-do optimism.

4. *Rigor:* Courage for hanging in there.
5. *Risk:* Courage for betting success on others.

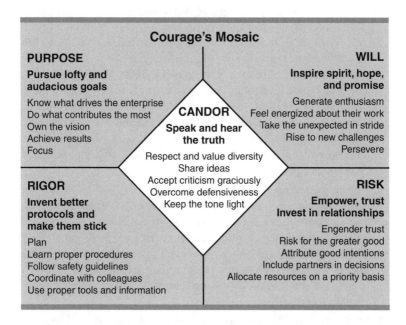

So how do these five factors unfold in the practice of leadership?

1. **Candor provides a foundation for courage.**
   Candor allows us to speak the truth to the powerful with a light touch, to listen nondefensively, to put ideas and options on the decision-making table respectfully, and to embolden our community. Leaders have occasion to speak with a prophet's voice, to act with candor. The prophet Nathan told the truth to King David in a pastoral story. Incensed by the injustice of the story of the theft of the prize lamb, the king's anger turned to shame and confession when he heard the words of Nathan: "You are the man!" (2 Sam. 12:7).

2. **Purpose gives us courage to pursue God-sized goals.**
   Purpose helps us stretch our community's horizons, to connect our hearts to God's goals, to stay focused until we get results, and to home in on a consistent vision. Think about the power of purpose. Jesus' was given a huge calling—redeem humankind—to complete in a brief ministry span of less than three years. He

charged his followers to complete the task: "go and make disciples of all nations" (Mt. 28:19).

3. **Will is the underpinning for our courage to persevere.**
Will awakens optimism and hope, creates "glue" for our community, reminds us to expect "crashes" and to learn from them, and reminds us to keep on keeping on. Imagine the audacity of the youthful David in the face of the giant Goliath: "You come against me with sword and spear and javelin, but I come against you in the name of the LORD Almighty…"(1 Sam. 17:45). Robert Jarvik, inventor of the artificial heart, reportedly claimed in an interview, "Leaders are visionaries with a poorly developed sense of fear and no concept of the odds against them." Leaders persist and keep on keeping on.

4. **Rigor puts structure into courage.**
Rigor builds consistency into our community, causes us to plan our work and work our plan, calls us to coordinate our ministry efforts and initiatives, and challenges us to inform each other seamlessly. Courage isn't just the oak's strength in the face of the storm. Courage is also embedded in the patience of the acorn. It waits under the snow for spring's warmth to help it grow into a mighty tree itself.

5. **Risk gives us the courage to bet our futures on others.**
Risk believes in the community, empowers others to act for and through the community, allocates the most resources to the best ministries, creates partners for tomorrow, and makes sacrifices for community progress.

For good or ill, modern warfare places the generals away from the actual front and makes command less personally perilous. Alexander the Great led armies in an extremely high-risk era of warfare. Battle was always intensely personal, with armies packed into rows for hand-to-hand combat. Force rather than finesse was the order of the day, and "he who dares wins" was the basic tactic. Soldiers stood shoulder-to-shoulder with their allies and fought face-to-face with their opponents. Because he was a first-over-the-wall general, Alexander was wounded dozens of times, so that as a mature man he was literally covered by the scars of old wounds.[7] Alexander shared the personal risk to life and limb with his troops. He took a stand and led by example.

As well as listing his own scars from risks he took for the gospel (2 Cor. 11:23–28), Paul bet his ministry on others. It's impressive to read Paul's risk takers' hall of fame in Romans 16.

- Phoebe, "a servant of the church" (vs. 1)
- Priscilla and Aquila, who "risked their lives for me" (vs. 4)
- Epenetus, "the first convert to Christ in the province of Asia (vs. 5).
- Mary, "who worked very hard for you" (vs. 6).
- Andronicus and Junias, "who have been in prison with me" (vs. 7).
- Ampliatus, "whom I love in the Lord" (vs. 8).
- Urbanus, "fellow worker in Christ" (vs. 9).

At least eighteen persons and households are noted in this chapter, along with the feats of faith for which each is remembered.

COACHING CONVERSATION

Courage is always an act of faith—faith in God and faith in the community. Practice faith—and leadership—dangerously.

COURAGE FREEZE-FRAMES FEAR

Courage propels us through our fears and toward our futures. It allows us to freeze-frame our fears and look at our functioning more objectively. The F-E-A-R acronym that follows charts one way to examine courage's opportunities when we're in deep water and need to face our fears.

- *F*-**Focus**—Courage reminds us to target "our attention on our intentions," and to ask, "What do I really want?"
- *E*-**Explore**—Courage helps us observe where our fear goes, downward to give us "cold feet," or upward to give us "hot heads." Courage allows us to confront ourselves with, "What's stopping me?"
- *A*-**Assess**—Courage pushes us to look at our options and assets and then to inquire, "What could I do?"
- *R*-**Respond**—Courage empowers us to choose and act and to clarify our actions with, "What will I do?"

Our community shrinks our fears and magnifies our courage as well. Leadership expert Warren Bennis observes, "Courage is a function of feeling part of a social fabric, of a network that's going to do something that has never been done before. People do gutsy things because they're in a group."[8]

Growing Challenges through Leadership: Vision

Vision is sighted.[9] It's "the art of seeing things invisible," according to Jonathan Swift, the seventeenth-century English satirist. Swift's definition echoes Scripture: "Now faith is being sure of what we hope for and certain of what we do not see" (Heb. 11:1). In fact, vision stretches our imaginations God-ward, weaving at least four types of sight into our congregation's futures.

Vision
is *foresight* into God's kingdom,
blessed by *insight* from God's Spirit,
illuminated by experience's *hindsight*, and
expanded by the *outsight* of needs beyond the congregation.[10]

STRETCHING IMAGINATIONS

God's futures for us stretch our imaginations. Given God's intention to redeem all mankind with eternity as his time horizon, his vision is much bigger and more imaginative than any mere human sight line. In contrast, traditional Industrial Age planning approaches tend to be straight-line projections. This style of visioning is heavily analytical, scientific, left-brained, and data-driven. Those methods are often a bit too mechanical to expand imagination, faith, and hope.

In general terms, visioning traditionally flows from three processes:

1. understanding the territory
2. generating a transforming perspective
3. transitioning from where we are to where we sense God is calling us

From territory, to transformation, to transition, that's the conventional approach to visioning.

But is the traditional approach to visioning imaginative and faith-full enough for a speeding world? Since humans and faith groups tend to grow either by pain or by challenge, this is our opportunity to step up and challenge our faith community. Begin with yourself. Stretch your imagination, and think more artistically about vision.

The future belongs to leaders who can cultivate the right-brain strengths of artistry, intuition, conceptualization, and emotion.[11] The ideas you're about to read will likely do one of two things for you as a visionary: confront you if you've relied too much on data, analysis, and logic; or balance you if you're willing to stretch your thinking style.

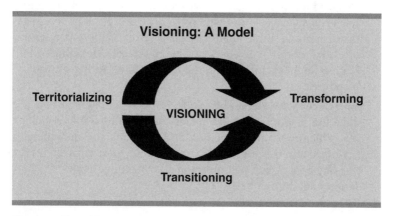

Visioning: A Model

Territorializing

VISIONING

Transforming

Transitioning

RAISING OUR HORIZONS

Let's stretch our redemptive imaginations.[12] Let me suggest four possibilities to enrich our visioning horizons–questions rather than data, metaphors rather than methods, intuitive responses rather than scientific analysis, and creative theological reflection about our futures rather than living from tradition. The first three are great warm-ups for breakthrough visioning of our congregation's futures. The fourth is foreign to many of us as leaders. It confronts us with how thoroughly we've been captured by scientific thinking and planning. Give a more artistic angle on vision an opportunity to open new lines of sight for you.

1. We can try to stretch our faithful imaginations by using "shot-in-the-light" questions (rather than "shot-in-the-dark" struggles) for congregational vision explorations. We offer our lives to God's kingdom and pray that it will come "down here" as it is "up there" (Mt. 6:10).
   - Where is God...?
   - What if...?
   - Where is God...?
   - What about...?
   - Where is God?

- How come...?
- Where is God...?
- What else...?
- Where is God...?

2. We can try to stretch our faithful imaginations by using metaphors to introduce new images into visioning processes. Lots of church leaders, especially those who were born and bred in congregational life and Bible studies, tend to give "right and religious answers" when involved in futuring processes. Metaphors allow leaders to back into Scripture rather than getting automatic responses.

Introduce future themes by asking, "How is our church like a..."? Take the responses to each image, build on how the metaphor resembles redemptive themes, and then link the metaphor to Scripture and theology. This process offers numerous angles for viewing congregational futures in a larger framework.

How is our church like a

- rescue squad?
- family reunion?
- pit crew?
- garden?
- maternity ward?
- yard sale?
- 24–hour restaurant?
- construction project?
- retreat center?
- beehive?
- coastline?

3. We can try to stretch our faithful imaginations by cultivating our intuitive ear for God. This approach draws on our inner, right-brain–or R-mode–voice that specializes in visual, spatial, and relational images.[13]

- Take a closer look at "accidents" and "coincidences." Believing is seeing. Is God speaking to you?
- Identify and cultivate your "inner receiver" and its signals. Does God use music, nature, friends, or other channels to speak to you?

- Give yourself the gift of quiet vision time each day. Can you tune out the static in your life so God can speak even in a whisper?

- Write down and review a journal of dreams and images. Like biblical characters, does God use your unconscious to speak to you?

- Look for "the question" that's being sharpened in you. Is God trying to get your attention by quietly raising an issue or theme repeatedly?

- Exercise the faith of a "guess" and deciding on partial information. Does God call you to act without guarantees?

4. We can try to stretch our faithful imaginations by reading the creation story with creator's eyes and applying those insights to our ministry vision. Read Genesis 1–3 carefully again for creative clues. Have you tried to think like an artist, thereby envisioning God's futures for you?[14] Are you willing to try? This fourth approach is a stretch for many of us, because it contrasts with traditional visioning and planning.

- **Look for the "edges."** Artists begin with edges, those places where two things meet or separate. This insight is apt to arise first in creative processes. To be understood and to be implemented, vision becomes focused.

  In Genesis, God created edges. He pushed back the chaos and used light and dark as well as land and sea for boundaries. What are the edges or boundaries for our congregation's future? Is there a new creative "day" or stage for our church? And, since the sun has oriented us from the beginning, where's your sun or your heliotropic source of power?

- **Watch for "space."** In art, space or ground is where things fit and fall into place. Ground helps identify what's "in" or "out," what's defined or left undefined.

  Vision is contextual. In Genesis, the creative context was "formless and empty" (Gen. 1:2). So, what's our space? What's our church's draw area? Who are the people groups we can reach? Where do opportunities and resources match for us? Without deliberate attention, this element of vision will likely remain invisible.

- **Observe "relationships."** Artists–and all of us–visualize things in relation to some constant element. What's unchanging? What lends perspective?

Vision has a benchmark. In Genesis, the Creator God was the constant. With a constant established, we can then more easily see proportions, comparisons, and angles. The law of simplicity pushes us to gather just enough information to identify a pattern—and no more. Our brains jump to conclusions when we "see" something familiar from our past catalog of things we "know."

This aspect of creativity is most difficult and often is unachieved. When we do visioning in faith communities, names make a difference and identify constants. What we give names and what we leave without names spotlights who we think is important and who's of no consequence. Mary Catherine Bateson poses a powerful question for us, "What would it be like to have not only color vision but culture vision, the ability to see multiple worlds of others?"[15] It requires real effort—and real vision—to identify the people who aren't usually on our radar screens.

• **Spot "lights."** In art, light is used to make things "look right." What's in the light rather than in shadowy background? What's visible and placed in the foreground? What sets the tone or mood?

In Genesis, creation came together and looked right when God pronounced it "good" (Gen. 1:4, 10, 12, 18, 21, and 25) and "very good" (Gen. 1:31). Vision spotlights what's real for us. What does our church highlight? What image does our church use to describe itself? What's real for us? This artistic touch is most likely to "connect the dots" for us and for others.

• **View "wholes."** Artists create patterns, gestalts, icons, symbols, and global perspectives. This insight is most magical and most unique. They look for what emerges when edges, spaces, relationships, and lights come together and unify. Artists look for connections and linkages. They pay attention to things that parallel or mirror each other. They watch for intersections, pivots, and centers.

Vision, like all things organic, sees the "big picture" and takes the "long view." In other words, creators—and leaders—look at the ocean as well as the waves. In the creation story of Genesis, the whole emerged when God completed both the natural and human creation. What is God's foundation for our church? What "makes sense" in community? When does our congregation "see" God's creation and respond?

Who's more creative than the Creator of the universe? Demographics and other analytical studies can help us understand some current circumstances, but only God can open the eyes of our imagination to his futures. Trust your intuition and spontaneity. Lead like an artist who "sees" new things, like an athlete who responds to the situation, like a jazz musician who improvises.

CHALLENGE SONGS FOR FAITH COMMUNITIES

Vision, to be made practical and real, is implemented in and through our faith communities. Our organic leadership model comes into play again here. John Shelton Reed,[16] expert on Southern culture, observes that to change a community, leaders can adopt a musical metaphor and take three actions–connecting, centering, and challenging–by:

1. **Connecting:** learning the "mother tongue" of the community.
   - Connect to the congregation and identify the base culture and values of the group and region. These provide a glossary to the mother tongue for the community.

2. **Centering:** tuning the community to a common key.
   - Gather the congregation around and center them in a compatible vision. Leaders craft a "stump speech," akin to politicians of an earlier time who jumped up on a stump and made their generic speech whenever a voter happened along. Make the stump speech brief, paint vivid word pictures, show intensity, personalize it by putting faces into the story, and repeat it again and again.
   - Think of creative ads or effective politicians or powerful preachers. They boil their message down to a phrase or a sentence, say it over and over, and give concrete examples of how people are changed by their idea. For example, some commentators consider the parable of the prodigal son the best story Jesus ever told. It's short, picturesque, emotional, personal, and in the familiar mother tongue. That's a masterful stump speech.

3. **Challenging:** singing the mother tongue in a minor key.
   - Challenge the congregation to advance. Know the ethos of the community, speak its language, have a sturdy connection

to the group, rally the group around a basic future, and use a minor key of the mother tongue to create a bit of dissonance to stretch the group's imagination and faith.

COACHING CONVERSATION

Speak directly—in the mother tongue. Listen. Take challenging stands—in the mother tongue. Leadership always has a "where": a setting, a culture. Understand "your brier patch," your longitude and latitude. Learn your community's heritage and genetic code, sing its "Zion songs," and hunger for its futures. Challenge the community from the inside—and from the perimeter.

✔ CASE STUDY: Matt's Challenges

Matt learned that the budget was his congregation's "hot button" issue. When the giving levels ran behind need levels, Matt's church got panicky. In the face of uncertainty, Matt decided to practice organic leadership. First, he tried to step back emotionally from the congregation's anxiety. He "coached" himself with two messages: I can't rescue the church's budget, and the deficit is not my fault. Then, Matt coached the budget committee in creative problem-solving and anxiety management. Whenever possible, he suggested the committee use a light touch with humor to help ease the tension in the church. Most importantly, Matt helped the budget committee present the facts and offer a clear challenge to the congregation to meet their giving deficits. He was pleasantly surprised at the response of the members to the committee's challenge.

Growing Intentional Revolutions

Challenging a community to do something new or to do something in new ways cultivates intentional revolutions.[17] What seeds can you sow that may sprout into substantive change? Jesus' ministry demonstrates broadly how he leavened his world, sowed fertile seeds, and called his followers to create a new world. The kingdom of God was and is an intentional revolution.

What do organic leaders do to cultivate intentional revolutions? Try these possibilities.

• Storytelling to awaken a different future. Jesus told parables of the kingdom to bring a new way of living and a richer future into focus.

- Partnering in a project to create a fresh reality. Jesus involved his followers in hands-on ministry to stretch their viewpoints and to show how love can change a world.

- Using the power of expectancy or self-fulfilling prophecy. Jesus built on the hope people had for messianic deliverance.

- Modeling how something is done. Jesus called his disciples, his learners, to preach, heal, and "be with him" (Mk. 3:14). He was a model of ministry and leadership.

- Creating new microclimates to reshape the relational environment. Jesus taught and forgave and bet his future on people who were consistently slow to see the kingdom. Yet after his death and resurrection, they turned the world upside down.

- Rewarding transformative behaviors. When Simon Peter jumped out of the boat (Mt. 14:29), he was given the ability to walk on the water, as Jesus did (at least until Peter's fear intervened).

- Pressing the point pointedly now and then. Without becoming coercive or willful, Jesus confronted the doubters with the "woes" of Matthew 23 and pushed his followers to risk more.

COACHING CONVERSATION

Congregations are volunteer organizations—but not many volunteer to change radically. There is nothing more revolutionary or intentional than the kingdom of God. Turn your face, like the sunflower, toward the kingdom. Lead toward the kingdom, and invite churches to follow along.

Power: The Ability to Do, a Radical Contrast

During the Industrial Age, leaders' power centered in formal authority, the organizational right to use leverage to make something happen. In a more organic framework, power is the leaders' ability to do something, and it bubbles up from an array of informal or formal sources. How power is described and applied is one of the sharpest contrasts between the fading industrial style of management and the organic approach to leadership.

Jesus announced the kingdom of God. But, it was an odd-sounding kingdom, since it had only servants and no king. Power was given away rather than hoarded. Conrad Hyers describes the servant spirit of the kingdom of God accurately: "the kingdom of God about which the Bible speaks is a kingdom that one enters, not like a king or at the right hand of a king, but on bended knee."[18] Jesus rarely exercised power or position over people. Hyers notes, "God moved through the pages of biblical history in third class."[19] There's encouraging news in that theme for organic leaders: God has shared his power with us. We are stewards of the power that flows from God's blessing and from our connections to the heart and heartbeat of the community.

In the industrial world, power was attached to titles and corner offices. Our emerging world empowers in other ways. What varieties of power are organic leaders endowed with? Leaders with courage and vision are empowered with at least five kinds of community power.

- *The power of "fellowship" and connection.* Leaders are community builders. There's power in people, the visibility of the public face of a faith community. One pastor of a large church described himself to me as "mayor," the primary preacher, teacher, prayer, and emcee of the congregation. Serving as community host and guiding ceremonial rituals is a quietly memorable and powerful role.

- *The power of "facilitation" and process.* Leaders know there's power in guiding community processes and helping progress occur. Growing trust and vision, discerning God's will, and coaching persons and groups are powerful "quiet" functions of leadership.

- *The power of "framing" and storytelling.* Leaders tell stories and shape ideas. They are positioned to know the community's deepest hopes and can give voice to those visions. They can keep the primary message in the foreground, define meaning, and create reference points.

- *The power of "first" and initiative.* Leaders set the pace for the community and take initiative. They embody vision, fill vacuums, front ideas, and "lead off." There's power in being first.

- *The power of "format" and structure.* Leaders recognize the importance of structure, routines, and patterns. They shape meetings, set agendas, and arrange settings. Each shapes the community's atmosphere.

COACHING CONVERSATION

You have a lot more power than you think. Use it strategically. Serve well. Become a steward of your leadership.

✔ **CASE STUDY: Matt Changed to Change**

Systems thinking helped Matt to see that faith communities change all the time, and yet change slowly. That discovery changed Matt's approach to change. He began by changing himself. Matt worked on developing more clarity about issues. He thought more before he spoke or acted. He concentrated on a simple but difficult behavior: calm and clear. In short, Matt learned the best way to challenge his congregation to change—challenge himself to change and grow. Organic leaders set the pace and show the way.

CHALLENGING COMMUNITIES HELIOTROPICALLY

Drawing power from a central source, like our sun, is an orienting metaphor for leaders and organic communities. It keeps us tracking our power and vitality supplier. What do "heliotropic" (or sun-oriented) leaders know and do?

Heliotropic leaders match needs to power.

Solar tracking plants are found in two broad varieties. Some face the sun and are called diaheliotropic. They maximize the solar radiation they receive. Others keep their backs to the sun and are termed paraheliotropic. They reduce the amount of solar radiation they receive. Desert annuals in particular show these behaviors. These plants can survive longer and better in inhospitable environs, because they reduce the temperatures and water evaporation rates of their leaves as the soil dries out. Leaders become aware that some of us thrive on light and others of us turn our backs on the light. Then, we match our needs to the available power sources.

Heliotropic leaders understand the rhythms of time.

The sun provides our basic sense of time as it rises and sets each day. Humans, animals, and plants have an internal sun-oriented clock. We refer to this clock as circadian rhythm, from the Latin *circa diem* or "about a day." In 1751, a Swedish botanist proposed using flowers as clocks.[20] He noted that dandelions perk up about 9 a.m., morning glories around 10 a.m., water lilies close to 11 a.m., chicory near 2 p.m., four o'clocks at (guess what?) 4 p.m., and evening primroses in the neighborhood of 6 p.m. Human health issues have a rhythmic pattern too. Heart attacks are more likely to occur in the morning, labor pains in the evening, and asthma difficulties at night. Time lends regularity to our lives and points us to seasonal cycles. We learn not to hurry the sun or try to delay it either.

Heliotropic leaders know that the hardiest seeds get a head start.

Sunflowers are often sprouted indoors before they are transplanted outdoors. The first seeds to sprout are apt to be the strongest and fastest growing plants in your garden. First, strongest, fastest—all of these qualities have great potential for health in communities.

Immunity Challenges

The health that emerges from our "suns" of identity and belief is the best challenge for communities' futures. Knowing who we are, understanding what we stand for, and drawing power from those sources offer us ways to turn our faces toward the sun's power and claim tomorrow. When we understand and value our community's center, we can then step to the edge of the system and challenge movement into our futures.

Pathogens may invade bodies and threaten health. They confront us with immunity challenges. These attackers have fewer advantages when our immune systems are strong and vigilant.

One More Time

The basic actions of organic leaders are connecting, centering, and challenging. That's what organic leaders do. We've explored how these foundational leadership actions are carried out. Visualize the elements, combinations, blends, and flow of organic leadership one more time in our model below.

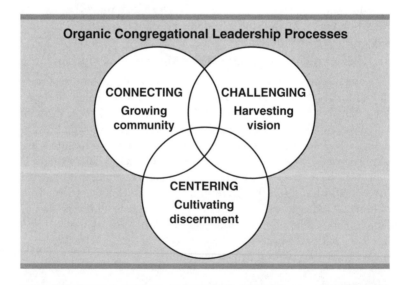

Organic Congregational Leadership Processes

CONNECTING
Growing
community

CHALLENGING
Harvesting
vision

CENTERING
Cultivating
discernment

Some Special Applications of Organic Leadership

We've charted the landscape of organic leadership both from the basic concept and the basic practices. Now let's look at some special applications in organic leadership—structure, strategy, and process.

PART 3

Harvesting Structures, Strategies, and Processes

A lot of leadership has invisible elements. Scientists study the invisible tectonic plates under the earth. In like manner, leaders are aware of and become stewards of some largely invisible forces to enhance the health of faith communities and to keep them immunized. Three of these—structure, strategy, and process—are generally taken for granted and rarely talked about in religious leadership. It's another of those common human triads.

As you read these final three chapters, think of the larger-scale, interwoven arrangements of people you try to lead. Remember that triads are the most common interactive pattern in human life. Can you see the triads in these classic relationships?

- For both strategy and structural reasons in human alliances, two or more link up because, "there's strength in numbers."

- Given the processes of human stress management, one takes the responsibility for two or more. No wonder we say, "The weight of the world is on my shoulders!"

- In the strategies and structures of human conflict, two are pitted against one. That makes "odd man out" conflict's favorite game.

- In the process of human marriage, two "become one flesh" (Gen. 2:24) and form an exclusive relationship to deal with outside triads.

In living organizations, three interacting forces interact and overlap:

- Leadership structure plays two roles: It dampens anxiety down and builds up sinew for ministry;

- Leadership strategy answers those crucial "which" and "when" questions about the community's direction and future;

- Leadership processes gather pools of community energy and channel them forward intentionally.

Taken together, these and other forces frame leadership for faith communities.

- Cultivating Leadership Structure
- Harvesting Leadership Strategy
- Planting Leadership Processes

CHAPTER 7

Cultivating Leadership Structures

Do you recognize the structure of the letter string below? Does it make any sense to you? Do you see the structure?

ETAONISRHDLUFCMWPGYBVKXJQZ

Code breakers tell us alphabets, like all living entities, assume shapes. What you see in the letter string above is the frequency distribution, from most used letters to least used ones, for the English language. That's an important pattern or structure for cryptographers to recognize. Even languages take on an inner structure.

Throughout the Industrial Age, structure was used to give shape to community life. Pyramids, hierarchies, departments, and compartments were the outgrowths of the mechanistic mind-set. In that tradition, structures were intended to stabilize, freeze, and preserve. In fact, we called these organizations "bureaucracies," named for the bureaus or chests full of paper they generated and preserved. Think of it. "Bureaucracy" means literally the rule of file cabinets, a state of mind the mechanistic age too often made the norm. That "preservation" mind-set doesn't serve us very well in dynamic eras of "blur" when flexibility is a necessity, although sometimes a maddening one.

Like most everything else, structures are morphing and changing in our era of history. Many types of structures have outlived their effectiveness. In reaction, some traditional organizations have flattened themselves and pushed authority upward or downward. Other organizations have become "virtual" by losing their edges and shifting their resources to their perimeters, relying on outsourcing. A third option is the network or "chaordic" (drawing its descriptive name from a combination of chaos and order) structure. Networked structures are difficult for traditional organizers to deal with since the whole doesn't know all the parts, the parts don't know the whole, and neither needs to. "Networks are frequently compared to 'self-organizing' biological systems in which the structure is determined by interaction among many autonomous agents, such as the individual members of a flock of migrating birds, rather than by predetermined plan and top-down leadership."[1] There are more–and simpler–structural options available to today's leaders than in earlier days. They can choose their structures for both flexibility and stability.

Flexible Stability and Stable Flexibility

"Communities have both a structure and a soul,"[2] affirms Rosabeth Moss Kanter. To put structure into more organic images, let's explore some ways to provide flexible stability or stable flexibility for growing things. A key leader balancing act is holding flexibility and stability in tension. Flexibility gives enough pliancy and elasticity to follow God in new, needed directions. Stability gives enough continuity and steadfastness to keep us from losing our faith moorings amid changes. Living things are both rooted and growing. They balance the exciting and frustrating tension of both flexibility and stability.

Living things self-organize into flexible but stable structures. Our religious heritage points to this very tension. During the Exodus and wilderness wanderings of the Old Testament, the Ark of the Covenant traveled in portable lodging, a tent. When the temple was finally built to permanently house the Ark, something was soon lost. God was seen to have a house, and then it was only a short mental journey to assume he was confined only to his temple. During the Exile, the Jews despaired that they were away from Jerusalem and, therefore, in their minds also away from God. They lamented, "By the rivers of Babylon we sat and wept / when we remembered Zion...How can we sing the songs of the LORD / while in a foreign land?" (Ps. 137:1, 4). Only with Ezekiel's vision of the wheel did Israel begin to realize God had never been limited by place. The prophet Jonah's voyage away from God's call dramatically taught him that God is an everywhere, everybody Redeemer.

Jesus' teachings about the kingdom of God in the New Testament continued to challenge believers to balance flexibility and stability. He called followers to a kingdom with no king or palace and to churches centered in people rather than places. Over time, progressing theologies have emphasized flexibility, and conserving theologies have insisted on stability. On the extreme ends of the believing spectrum, most of the flexible stability and stable flexibility have been lost or limited.

Creation's Unique Designs

Creation structures itself in arcs, cascades, spirals, and helixes–an entire array of patterns with surprises. To identify one instance of uniqueness, honeysuckle is one of the few climbing plants that twines leftward. Still, God's most elementary creations–the insect and animal worlds–offer clues for selecting our leadership of structures. Let's begin with some of the simplest creatures of all–termites.

If nature gave awards for structural engineering, the termite would win every time. I'm not talking about wimpy North American termites, the little insects that mainly lunch on our houses. The master architects among critters are the African and Australian termites. They construct nests that are the human equivalent of 180-story buildings–roughly 2000 feet high by human measure, or what would be the tallest building in the world. That's not bad for a tiny insect. But more importantly for our purposes, termites build smart structures as well as large ones. Creatively, we can learn from how they design their "termitaries," or termite mounds:

- Using local materials
- Designing for single-system construction and development
- Producing nothing that's toxic to the system
- Creating curved shapes for strength
- Building for maximum space
- Reducing waste in motion and material
- Making livable spaces

Three million insects may live together in a single termite mound. They build their homes from the most elemental materials–local soil and saliva. The hard, thick walls seal moisture inside and keep heat outside. They create channels and ducts to circulate air, creating a heating and air conditioning system that circulates air using only the natural convection forces of heat, cold, and gravity. In some desert settings, the termites sink tunnels down to ground water supplies, another source of cooling for the interior of the mound. In rainy climates, an umbrella-like roof directs water away from the mound. They adapt to their challenges and structure their lives and homes accordingly.

COACHING CONVERSATION

Let structure emerge that is adapted to fit local needs, is tailored to local resources, is healthy for the community, can be maintained by the community, and is good stewardship for the community. Where structure is concerned, one size doesn't fit all.

Learning from Creation

Creation's clues for structure come from a variety of phenomena discussed below:

- growing seasons, the lessons of timing
- hardiness zones, the lessons of matching seeds and settings
- local microclimates, the lessons of nuanced opportunities
- skeletal systems, the lessons of support and connections
- life stages, the lessons of maturing
- life transitions, the lessons to be learned when bad things happen to good communities
- change dynamics, the lessons of turbulence
- grafting processes, the lessons of uniting multiple organisms
- the "math" of community mission, the lessons of types of congregations

These are "yeasty" classrooms, but not necessarily the old familiar industrial or traditional ones.

Congregational Seasons: Timing's Structures

"Season" is an organic idea. The word comes from the Latin for "to sow" and refers to sowing time. When expanded to include all four of the seasonal rhythms of a year, "seasons" suggest ways to structure leadership. What do the actions of good gardeners suggest to you as a strategic leader? What can you do to think and act "seasonally" in your leader role?

Spring—Structures for Germinating New Ministry Ventures

Spring is the season for planting, transplanting, grafting, and seeding new efforts. Plants and animals leave dormancy behind and begin to grow again in the warming weather of spring. Gardener-leaders

- prepare deep, rich seedbeds
- choose lots of great seeds and plantings
- sow seeds at optimum times
- give extra nurture to new seedlings
- take advantage of the sun

COACHING CONVERSATION

Plan, prepare, and plant new ministries carefully. New ministries, like most living things, are most fragile when they're newborns. However, nurturing new life is exciting work for organic leaders.

Summer—Structures for Growing Ministries

Summer is the season to make the most of growth spurts. It is, after all, the warmest time of the year and is most hospitable to expansion. Gardener-leaders

- cultivate carefully
- feed and fertilize as needed
- thin plants and weed out competition
- water as required

COACHING CONVERSATION

Protect growing ministries carefully. Serve as a steward of promise, and don't stifle momentum. This is the make-or-break time and the season of greatest growth and change.

Fall—Structures for Harvesting Ministries

Fall is the season for maturing, reaping, and consolidating the yield of a growing cycle before decline sets in. In most cases, we reap what we've sown. We put our energies into growing things and, as a result, we grow ourselves. Gardener-leaders

- harvest crops as they ripen
- disturb the seedbed as little as possible
- save the best seeds for planting next year
- leave organic matter on seedbeds to feed next year's crop

COACHING CONVERSATION

Preserve the yield of your labors. This is the time to celebrate a good crop. Look at the variety of seeds or approaches you used. Evaluate which grew best and yielded most.

Winter—Structures for Dormant Ministries

Although some grains are planted in the fall for spring harvest, winter is generally the season for resting, readying, and planning another ministry cycle during the least hospitable times for growth. Gardener-leaders

- plow organic matter into seedbeds to enrich next year's growing culture
- run soil tests and plan to amend any deficits
- repair and sharpen tools for another growing season
- phase out crops that have served their purpose
- decide which fields need a fallow season
- do research on promising new options
- prune trees during dormancy
- prepare for grafting

COACHING CONVERSATION

Living things require rest, respite, and time to gather themselves for a new season. Observe sabbath, dormancy, and hibernation. Anticipate new ventures and plan for them now.

Congregational Growing Zones: Matching Structures

Imagine yourself in a garden shop in the spring. You're looking for some plants to add color and curb appeal to your front yard. But, you're not sure what will grow the best in your region. Then you spot it. "It" is a map of North America with eleven color-coded zones meandering across the landscape. You've discovered "growing zones," a guide to what grows where.

Growing zones, also called hardiness zones or climate zones, help you customize plantings to suit the climate of your specific region. Based on the average coldest temperatures for your area, the standard map is provided by the United States Department of Agriculture and graphs out eleven zones.[3] Zone 11 is the warmest region and takes in Hawaii as well the southernmost region of Florida. Zone 1 is the coldest zone, charting the northernmost latitudes and the highest elevations. Most of us live and grow someplace between the extremes.

Congregations have their own unique growing zones or comfortable temperatures as well. Good leaders, like good gardeners, study the hardiness zones of their communities. They discover some patterns about what will grow where.

- Some faith communities can stand more heat than others. They have learned over time that structure helps humans deal with anxiety. These churches have built in some coping approaches so they react less to conflict situations. They can "take the heat."

- Other churches have mastered the art of the "cold shoulder." They threaten to freeze out any member who gets out of line. It can get awfully frosty in these climates for both members and leaders.

Of course, the point is that not much grows in environments that are either too hot or too cold. The wise gardener learns what grows where and sets out lots of plants suited to the setting. Knowing your garden's hardiness zone is the beginning point for good growing.

COACHING CONVERSATION

Understand the hardiness zones of your congregation. Then you'll know what grows where. It gets really tricky when you find you have more than one hardiness zone in your church, a highly likely prospect. The good news is that more zones means you have more growth options.

Congregational Microclimates: Nuanced Structures

Not all weather is created equal. In fact, our world is a jigsaw puzzle of microclimates.

A microclimate is the climate of a small area that's distinct from the area surrounding it. Whether warmer or colder, wetter or drier, windier or calmer, it's different than its near neighbors. Some microclimates are small—like an area protected by a building. Other microclimates are larger—such as the Chicago shoreline along Lake Michigan, where the water moderates temperatures all year long.

The most common microclimates we see in our daily lives are large bodies of water, urban areas, and slopes. Lakes, sounds, and oceans tend to keep winter temperatures from becoming as extreme, extending the growing season. Urban areas tend to absorb more daytime heat into their buildings and pavements, moderating night and winter lows. By the same token, buildings provide shelter from winds. In fact, urban areas may be a full "hardiness zone" warmer than nearby rural areas. Of course, that extra heat can be unwelcome to people and plants during heat waves. Slopes provide lots of lessons about topographical microclimates. Since cold air is heavier than warm air, it, like water, flows downhill and pools in low areas. On winter nights, some valleys may be ten degrees colder and, therefore, more prone to frost than their higher neighbors. In contrast, hilltops may remain slightly warmer but suffer from exposure to winds. Slopes facing the south receive more direct sun and warm up more quickly in spring than their north-facing neighbors.

Does your yard have microclimates? Yes, it does. Your house, fences, and walls shelter your yard from prevailing winds and create warmer and more sheltered microclimates, generally on southern and eastern sides. The tradeoff is that these same south and east facing areas are probably more exposed to the baking rays of summer sun. Turbulence from wind blowing around the more sheltered corners of your house may also have a drying effect on trees, shrubs, and plantings. Of course, you know that already; you've noticed a fan fools your skin into thinking the air is ten to fifteen degrees cooler than summer temperatures really are. Paved areas gather more heat and shunt away rainwater, and heavy clay-based soils act like pavement in some cases, making them less hospitable to certain plants. Microclimates may explain why you've had better luck with some plants in some places in your yard than you could account for readily.

Leaders understand the microclimates of their congregation. Some plants thrive in exposed areas, and some church members prefer challenge, risks, and even hardship. Other plants need sheltered areas, and some church members require careful protection as well. Leaders recognize that what's adjacent to growing things may influence the degree to which full growth can occur in neighboring areas.

COACHING CONVERSATION

Sometimes it takes two or three seasons to fully grasp the different microclimates inside a community. Watch, experiment, and learn. Different situations call for different strategies. Match ministries to conditions.

Congregational Skeletons: Supportive Structures

We humans have a framework of 206 bones to provide structure for our bodies. Our spine is the central axis, with seven cervical vertebrae in the neck, twelve thoracic vertebrae in the trunk of the body, and another five lumbar vertebrae in the lower back. Our skulls rest at the top of our spines, and our pelvises are attached to the lower spinal area. Our limbs are appended to our bony frames, and our joints connect neighboring bones. Most joints are movable, like our arms and legs. Our bones are held together by flexible bands of connective tissues called ligaments.

Skeletons are supportive structures. Literally meaning a dried body, our skeletons buttress our tissues and protect our vital organs. Leaders take advantage of the support structures of congregational life, especially "connective" tissues of the body of Christ. The living ligaments of a congregation give both strength and "bend" to Christ's body; they connect important functions in the community. And, the value of folks who are the heart or eyes of the congregation are crucial to the community as well and sometimes need the protection of leaders for the health of the body.

COACHING CONVERSATION

Keep the axis of the body of Christ strong and flexible. It carries the weight of the physical and organizational body[4] and supports the core for health and resiliency.

Congregational Life Stages: Maturity Structures

Life—both for individuals and groups, for plants and animals—moves through fairly predictable stages and phases.[5] As a rule, younger communities are usually more flexible but structurally unstable, and older communities are generally more stable but structurally inflexible. Younger communities need stability because, like babies, they can't walk very well. They're too unsure on their feet. On the other hand, older communities need flexibility because, like senior adults, they can't bend easily. Additionally, older people and older congregations may also be "sclerotic," showing a hardening of the categories.

COACHING CONVERSATION

Maturity, either in life or faith, changes us. Keeping a healthy balance between flexibility and stability is a constant challenge for us and for our communities. That balancing act refocuses stage-by-stage as we mature. Younger churches need foundations and anchors. Older churches need hinges and buoys.

Congregational Rehabilitation: Transitional Structures

A friend of mine claims structure gives him "a track to run on." He's right. That's one of the practical functions of any structure and a basic human need. But, how do we respond when our lives get derailed?

I like the structural image of our churches as halfway houses. Most of us—and most of our communities—face seasons of healing and transitioning. *Rehabilitation,* meaning to qualify us again or to outfit us anew, is a basic concept for lives that get broken or bent from time to time. To see the church as a halfway house for transitions or as a supply tent for supplying the troops for a new foray into the world is a powerful symbol of faith communities. The combination of stability and flexibility is spiritual and emotional manna for us as believers in the midst of life's passages. Halfway houses are temporary habitats where we rehab ourselves for fresh futures.

Humans want home bases. We're hungry to relate to like-minded groups with futures. (That's another way of saying we want to be connected, to be centered, and to be challenged.) That's especially true when life goes awry. Pay attention to transitions in persons and communities. Transitions are times when we earn our spurs as leaders. During transitions, systems open up like flowers to the sun during significant turning points, or close up like a turtle retreating into its shell. Encourage the flowers, and comfort the turtles.

Congregational Turbulence: Change Structures

The uncertainty of constant change has been described as permanent white water.[6] The chaos of the rapids threatens to overwhelm our leaders. But, some observations about the nature of frothy rapids may offer clues to structuring our living congregations and leadership behaviors. White-water kayakers have developed squirt boats. Shaped like potato chips or high-tech wings, they barely touch the water, skimming or squirting through the turbulence. These new boats require a different kind of boater.

Unlike earlier folks who mainly shot the rapids by brute force and good fortune, sucking it up and riding the waves in headlong plunges, today's kayakers are more apt to read the water. They have noted that white water has two dynamics:

1. the mainstream of water cascading more or less straight over the rocks
2. eddies along the margins or riverbanks

These eddies offer a place for boaters to pause and choose a course before diving back into the core of the riverbed for another leg of the downward quest. Seasoned kayakers use the swirling eddies to rest, gather themselves physically and emotionally, and study the patterns of current. They read the river and play the river by slowing or stopping or drifting as they choose their next steps. They enjoy the adventure of the river as well as the satisfaction of reaching their destination.

In an all-white-water world, use—or create—eddies along your path. Be thoughtfully deliberate, especially in a hurried situation. Gather yourself, and calm your mind. Keep your focus. Acknowledge and enjoy the froth, but don't be distracted by it. Amid turbulence, slow down and think.

Congregational Multiplication: Grafting Structures

The prophet spoke poetically of the way Israel had sprouted from the stump or stock of Jesse, using what's left after the ax cuts down the trunk of the tree (Isa. 11:1). He was describing the natural sprouting that happens when shoots spontaneously grow from stumps that still have a root system. That's a natural phenomenon. But, grafts can create intentional mergers of two or more plants. That's a fertile structure for leaders to consider.

Grafting is the art and science of joining two or more living things together. Using plants as our model here[7], apple trees can, for example, be grafted to produce multiple varieties of apples. Grafting trees unites a new top with a mature trunk. This process combines an upper graft, or a scion, with the lower portion, or the understock, providing the trunk and root system. There are several structural lessons from grafting plants that offer counsel for leaders who are considering mergers or partnerships:

- Plants of closely related botanical forms can usually be grafted successfully.
- Grafts of plants may produce new growth but not new varieties.
- Poor grafts result in weak, fragile, or dying plants.
- Grafting requires timing. Plant grafts are usually done in late winter or early spring before new growth begins.
- Plants chosen for grafting are usually about the same size. In any event, scions should not be larger than understock.
- New grafts call for careful cut-and-fit matches and wrapping or waxing to reduce drying.
- New growth from grafts are groomed but never pruned heavily.

In a networking and partnering culture, grafting is a natural structural option for leaders to consider. Multiply your impact by linking with other communities of common cause and passion. Take time to test compatibility. Networks require constant cultivation. It's a simple lesson: More impact takes more effort.

Congregational Arithmetic: Missional Structures

Community Conversations

The Industrial Age defined capital primarily as money. More recently, capital has been reframed as "social capital," our common sense of belonging, and "wisdom capital," the accumulated stories that are passed along generation to generation. The radical shift is from cash to community. Meaning and memories, those experiences that glue communities together, make "common sense," or sense in community. Meaning and memories are community's common ground.[8]

No longer is a community just a matter of geographic proximity. In a webbed world, leaders are more likely to describe community by what we believe rather than where we live.[9] Community is the context in which we tell our stories, share our lives, and talk together.

The current debates about capital cause our communities sometimes—deliberately or accidentally—to define ourselves "mathematically" in relation to our sense of and pursuit of mission. Think of the basic math operations you learned in elementary school, and apply those types of math to the structures and ethos of your faith community.

- **Additive Community Structures**—Some groups major on health by addition, by reaching out to like-minded folks. They increase their outreach, extend their scope, and amplify their mission deliberately.

- **Subtractive Community Structures**—Some communities are high-focus, one-track, tightly bounded groups. These groups have a narrow mission, and distractions to their health and well-being aren't welcome. They sift the wheat from the chaff and reduce their purposes by design.

- **Multiplicative Community Structures**—Some communities are partnerships. These networks recognize that the many can accomplish things that a person isn't capable of doing singly. They know their influence and health are increased geometrically by widening their network of alliances.

• **Divisive Community Structures**–Some groups define themselves by what they're against, contrasting themselves with their larger communities. These special interest groups find their reason for being in correcting, advocating for, or reversing a particular problem. They separate and partition themselves from others by categories as a way to defend their community's health as they define it.

This math of community life can be sorted and depicted around two larger-scale dynamics: positive and negative missions, simple and complex structures.

	POSITIVE MISSION	NEGATIVE MISSION
SIMPLE STRUCTURE	Additive Communities	Subtractive Communities
COMPLEX STRUCTURE	Multiplicative Communities	Divisive Communities

• **Positive-negative.** The more positive communities–the additive and multiplicative ones, those who are relationship-based–are apt to be more theologically centrist with broader congregational agendas. The more negative communities–the subtractive and divisive ones, those who are issue-oriented–are more likely to be on the ends of the theological poles where more predictable emotions rule. The extreme left end of the theological spectrum often operates on anger; they try to make their communities more "metro" and up-to-date. The extreme right end of the theological spectrum frequently is activated by fear; they retreat into "retro" communities and try to recreate traditions.

• **Simple-complex.** The simpler communities–the additive and subtractive ones–operate by straightforward guidelines. The additive communities want "more" and the subtractive communities want "ours." The more complex communities–the multiplicative and divisive ones–are diverse entities with clusters of sub-groups.

What's your community's DNA? How does your congregation "do math"? How do you lead your distinctive blend of structures?

✔ **CASE STUDY: Matt Uses Structure to Ease Anxiety**

Applying family systems' approaches to pastoral leadership changed Matt's way of working with structure. Early in his ministry, he had used structure as a lever. For him, there were right and wrong ways to organize programs and ministries. When he discovered organic leadership, Matt began to see that structure is one way to dampen congregational anxiety. People like to understand the flow of processes and know what to expect. Matt learned to appreciate flexibility as well as stability.

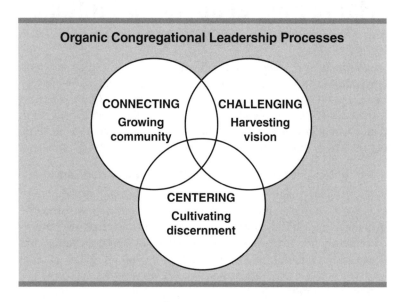

Organic Congregational Leadership Processes

CONNECTING
Growing
community

CHALLENGING
Harvesting
vision

CENTERING
Cultivating
discernment

From Structure to Strategy

Now let's move to another largely invisible ingredient of organic leadership: strategy. Like structure and process, it's not a commonly discussed issue in religious leadership.

CHAPTER 8

Harvesting Leadership Strategy

Strategy is a basic stewardship in leadership. Since our faith communities rarely have all of the resources or time or people we need, strategy answers "which" and "when" questions. Organic leaders learn what to center in and focus on. Organic leaders learn how to plant, when to cultivate, and when to harvest. Leaders who think organically attune themselves to the importance of strategic ministry.

Focus, Flexibility, Futures: Roots, Wings, Horizons

A popular greeting card says we give our children first roots and then wings. Actually, if we parent strategically and well, we probably provide our children roots, wings, and then horizons. We parents help them find a life focus, grow and adjust to new discoveries, and move into their futures. The parallel is obvious. If congregational leaders think and act strategically, that strategy provides roots, wings, and horizons, too.

In essence, strategy encourages us to find our center, our strengths, and our advantages. Strategy helps us lead from our points of excellence. Unfortunately, strategy isn't always explored in leadership development and is even less considered by religious leaders. How can we fill this gap? How can we learn to be better strategists as organic leaders?

Looking at the way artisans hone their craft offers religious leaders one beginning point. Artisans learn strategy[1] by chiseling away all of the marble that doesn't match their statue, by painting on a blank canvas until the picture they have in their heads appears, and by writing words and music on a page until they and others hear the song that's in their imaginations. Jesus probably deepened his strategic gifts in the carpentry shop. There he envisioned the table his customer wanted. Then, he cut down a tree that contained that specific table, cured planks until he had the lumber he needed for that table, and shaped and planed materials into the unique table that had been ordered. Strategists learn to look long-term and wide-angle for "which" and "when" issues.

On-the-Run Strategy Development

Rosabeth Moss Kanter draws a powerful example from the world of theater about how strategy works in our age of blur. She claims the Industrial Age fostered strategy as traditional theater. There were pre-written scripts, actors with assigned roles, and words that were recited the same way every time the play was done. It was a "no surprises," perfect-plan-in-advance, "I'll-know-it-when-I-see-it" world.

But, she reminds us, "Times of uncertainty call for improvisation."[2] Our day requires improvisational theater–a general theme, actors who develop the story as they go, and a play that's likely to improve with every performance. Like another art form, jazz, today's strategists establish a firm direction and then enjoy playing variations on the theme. It's an experimental and experiential "I'll-see-it-when-I-know-it" attitude.

Kanter offers six seeds for a more organic approach to developing leadership strategy. You, as an organic leader, can build on these seeds:

1. *Theme*–a mission statement, a description of vision and values, a focus to establish a baseline;
2. *Theater*–a stage for action, a place to rehearse possibilities, an incubator;
3. *Actors*–people with faith and discipline to act without full information in advance;
4. *Drama and Suspense*–a sense that resolution is on the way, the knowledge that we all look like geniuses after the fact when clearer direction emerges;
5. *Audiences*–interaction and involvement with others more than attention to mere reaction;
6. *Successive Versions and Variations*–test and revise, try and trash, launch and learn.

For those of us who have been steeped in a more scientific approach, an advance plan is comfortable. The problem we've always faced is the wild card, the discovery that surprises are everywhere and that our futures are not in our hands. We've tried to fail fast and learn better ways. The speed of our world forces us to improvise more and more. Fortunately, religious leaders have a strategy book to use for guidance for this way of leading.

Focus, Flexibility, Future

The New Testament unfolds a simple flow of strategic thinking and acting for us to follow. This flow is the essence of the strategic process in the New Testament and in leadership[3] :

Organic Leaders Focus with Flexibility on the Future

FOCUS

In the Gospels, Jesus focused on the kingdom of God as the central pursuit in believers' lives. More than eighty times, Jesus mentioned the kingdom of God (or the kingdom of heaven). It was the most common theme in his unforgettable stories, the parables. It's clear that God's kingdom was the anchor idea in Jesus' life and ministry. It was his vision and his mission. He lived, ministered, and died for the kingdom of God.

Core beliefs anchor the baseline for strategists. That central concept, that force of gravity that pulls everything to center provides a measuring stick for progress and a destination depot for arrival. It's the hill we're willing to die on. Religious leaders make this focal point deeply theological. It's a matter of faith, practice, and health. Core beliefs stabilize us.

COACHING CONVERSATION

Remember Martin Luther's "here I stand" bottom line? "Unless I am convicted by Scripture and plain reason—I do not accept the authority of popes or councils, for they have contradicted each other—my conscience is captive to the Word of God. I cannot and I will not recant anything, for to go against conscience is neither right nor safe."[4] That's focus. Get back to basics—then take them forward organically.

FLEXIBILITY

In the Book of Acts, the kingdom of God still was the foundation for all they did in ministry. However, they also cultivated flexibility in the face of two unique happenings–persecution for their faith, as well as the revolutionary opportunities the Holy Spirit opened to them. They focused on the kingdom with flexibility.

Organic leaders know living things can't be controlled, and always have an element of unpredictability built in. When I overseed fescue in my lawn each year, I notice the tag on the seed bag lists a specified percentage of "other," meaning there will be surprise plants among the blades of fescue the next spring and summer. God's surprises are part of leadership. It's one of the ways he challenges us to see and act beyond our comfort zones.

In our natural world, beaver dams are interesting examples of focus with flexibility. Beavers build sturdy lodges, working underwater for up to fifteen minutes, a handy trait for hydro-engineering. Beginning with heavy logs at the bottom, they create tepee-shaped structures with living chambers of three to six feet for entire beaver families. These chambers are situated a few inches above water level and can be entered through any one of several underwater tunnels. The lodges are sealed with mud and plant material but have vents to supply fresh air. Plumes of steam, created by the body heat from the hibernating beaver family, rise from the vents in the winter.

Beavers want their own house. That's the strategic focus for lodge builders. Yet occasionally threats confront their lodges' futures. Sometimes the water level drops, and the beaver dams have to be repaired. But the most troublesome threat occurs when the water levels rise. This dilemma opens two options. Either the dam has to be lowered, or the chamber floor has to be built up. That's when you see the strategic flexibility and ingenuity of the beaver building crews.

COACHING CONVERSATION

It's easy for leaders to lose balance. Either they lock into their focus and ignore the Holy Spirit's invitations to advance in novel directions, or they chase every fad and sacrifice all focus. Become a rare leader who maintains focus while remaining flexibly open to God's new work. Staying focused and centered allows organic leaders to improvise as God's Spirit leads us along the way.

FUTURE

Leaders are future-oriented. Paul, like most of the pioneering Christian leaders, kept a future-oriented perspective early in his ministry (Phil. 3:12–14). So it's a bit surprising that only a couple of generations downstream from Jesus, the early church had already begun to defend and conserve its traditions. The Pastoral Letters of Timothy and Titus, the first pastor's handbook, have a noticeably protective tone. Listen to the reactive tone of these statements.

- "Guard the good deposit that was entrusted to you" (2 Tim. 1:14).
- "straighten out what was left unfinished" (Titus 1:5).
- "hold firmly to the trustworthy message as it has been taught…and refute those who oppose it" (Titus 1:9).
- "rebuke them sharply, so that they will be sound in the faith" (Titus 1:13).

The basic risk in holding onto the past is that you may forfeit the future. That's the surprising time horizon of the Pastorals. Strategists focus with flexibility–on the future. To ignore the future is to lose leadership and to become a caretaker.

Gardeners recognize that time horizons are crucial in planting and growing decisions. For instance, flowers have essentially three time horizons. Annuals complete their life cycle–they sprout, grow, flower, and produce seed–in one growing season. Other flowers are biennials, producing leaves their first season and blooms the second one. Sweet William and foxglove are examples of plants that have two-year life cycles. Perennials are plants that live year after year. While the tops of these plants die back with freezing conditions, they grow from their roots each spring. Some gardeners enjoy reinventing their flowering beds every season, but others prefer the continuity of perennials. It's a strategic decision related to shorter-term or longer-term time horizons. It's a matter of which future you prefer and need.

COACHING CONVERSATION

Roots and wings are important, but time horizons are crucial too. It isn't enough to play defense alone and try to preserve a past. Even a 0–0 score is still a tie at best.[5] Settling for ties isn't good enough to keep communities healthy and afloat.

Gravity Rules

Water is the most abundant substance on earth. Covering 71 percent of Earth's surface, water's reflection is the reason we're called the "blue planet." Our hydrosphere, the water component of the earth, is immense. Water is everywhere and in everything. On a personal level, nearly two-thirds of the human body is water. On an atmospheric level, bodies of water retain heat, making our oceans into huge heat reservoirs. Temperature varies only one-third as much in oceans as they do on land, creating microclimates along the milder coastal zones.

Water may be the majority, but gravity rules. Look at tides. Ocean tides reflect gravity's pull from the moon and sun. Where the moon is nearest to earth, our oceans actually "bulge" or distort and pile up toward the moon, causing tidal movements. (Oddly enough, there's another bulge, or, more correctly, there's a "sag," on the opposite side of the earth too, because the earth blocks some of the moon's gravitational force. For every tug toward change, there's usually a resistance to that change.) As the earth rotates on its axis daily and as the moon cycles around us monthly, gravity causes the tides to rise and fall.

Gravity, that attraction that holds the universe together, is impossible to explain fully. But, its effects are easy to see. Gravity keeps the planets in orbit, causes unsupported objects to fall to the ground, and creates tidal rhythms. Gravity is invisible, but its impact through phenomena like ocean tides is obvious. In leadership terms, gravity pulls us to center and is purposive and powerful. Center gives us direction, and then strategy empowers us to map the trail ahead for us.

COACHING CONVERSATION

Your center of gravity literally holds you together and provides focus and self-definition. A professional singer told me how crucial balance is in high-quality vocal production. He described how he took care to establish a solid foundation or footing and balance himself before he hit his first note. First, he found his center of gravity, and then, he sang. Religious leaders are well advised to do the same in Christ. You can't stand or take a stand without your sense of gravity.

From Where We Are to Where God Wants Us to Be

Strategists help us move from where we are to where God wants us to be. So, where are we? Theological futurists looking for historic clues ask an intriguing question: Is our century more like the first century than any era since? If the answer is yes, how do we respond to God?

How do our century and the century of Christ and Paul compare? How are the first and twenty-first centuries alike? Let me offer seven comparisons for you to consider.

The Two Eras—First and Twenty-first Centuries— Are Both Reflective of

- Fast-Changing Times
- Periods of Cultural Chaos
- Nonscientific Mind-sets
- Global Outlook and Awareness
- Eras of "Spirit" and Mystery
- Hostility to Faith's Perspectives
- Churches with Infectious Faith

Think about it. There was a contagious movement afoot in first-century Christianity. When persecution pressured and scattered Christ's faithful followers from their home base in Jerusalem, a missionary spirit swept faith across the known world. It was a "holy spirit" that energized the church. In fact, the Holy Spirit is mentioned more than forty times in the first half of the Book of Acts alone. This movement of Christ's Spirit turned the world upside down—in only one-third of a century. It's an amazing story to read, think about, and wonder about. How does a worldview spread like a prairie fire? How can a culture change so radically and so rapidly? Can such a movement of God happen again and again?

Maybe we haven't thought big and bold enough. Michelangelo pushed us to look on our world from wider angles: "The greater danger for most of us is not that our aim is too high and we miss it, but that it is too low and we reach it." Or, to apply a more contemporary dare, the dedication from *The Prayer of Jabez* challenges us: "To all who—like those Christians in the book of Acts—look at who they are now and who they'll never be, and what they can do now and what they'll never be able to do…and still ask God for the world."[6] The leaders of Acts—those who were spotlighted as well as those who remained unnamed—lived and believed large. They knew their faith was contagious.

Contagious Ideas

Christianity is a contagious idea. Or, as C. S. Lewis described it, a "good infection."[7] Lewis saw Christ's incarnation as planting a contagion that continues to germinate and spread. Sadly, we may have settled for less than contagion. The Industrial mind-set tended to shrink change down into manageable increments rather than the sweeping trans-formational movement of Acts. Acts challenges us toward orders of change rather than simple degrees of change. Acts doesn't ask us: "Do we have faith?" Instead, Acts confronts us: "Does faith have us?" That's the transformational movement issue. Is our faith catching?

Christianity is a "viral" idea, a contagious concept. Contagious ideas are "memes,"[8] the cultural equivalent of biological genes.

LEADER'S LEXICON

"Memes," the phenomenon that ideas have their own momentum and spread uncontrollably through populations.

They fit our lives and sweep through groups. Like all epidemics, contagious ideas have carriers or hosts, plus infected groups or host populations. For those of us who are believers, it's no stretch to see faith as a viral concept. But what do nonreligious people think are the contagious seeds in Christianity?

Christianity's "Stickiest" Memes

From essentially an outside perspective, Aaron Lynch identifies four memetic ingredients that make Christian faith contagious:[9] the power of passionate proselytizing, the lure of loving concern, the magnetism of bold belief, and the appeal of memorable symbols.

1. **The "go and preach the Gospel to all" meme**
   The contagion of passionate proselytizing caused early Christianity to spread quickly. Despite the losses of its founder and many of its earliest leaders to heavy persecution, Christianity became a faith movement. When "carrier-leaders" are being eliminated, only rapid growth can create "movement-rate" expansion.

2. **The "love" meme**
   The contagion of loving concern leavens fear and uncertainty by swaying the not-quite-persuaded to feel proselytism is for their personal good. Love-in-action increases emotional receptivity to belief and makes new carriers more likely to pass the "good

infection" along. When I was pastor of a campus church, a cult reached several members from our congregation by showing more concern during a personal or life crisis than the church itself had done. It was a painful and unforgettable lesson in strategic leadership. Love is always in season.

3. **The "cross" meme**

The contagion of bold belief is particularly powerful. Believers owe everything–especially their eternal salvation–to the one who suffered and died for them. Therefore, enormous sacrifices–missionary service, direct evangelism, and risky ministry–become ways to repay the costs of the cross.

4. **The "ritual" meme**

The contagion of memorable symbols provides emotional adhesive for believers. These rituals have a broad range of symbolic activities–enacting ceremonies like weddings, funerals, baptisms, and the Lord's Supper; setting confessions and memories to song; wearing religious objects such as crosses or "WWJD" bracelets; saying prayers before meals or at bedtime; wearing distinctive religious garb; displaying biblical images in stained glass or art; joining in the life of a faith community.

Tipping Points of Epidemics

What does it take for an idea or action to reach critical mass and take on momentum on its own? When does contagion become an epidemic, a movement? How does a viral idea arrive at its tipping point?

LEADER'S LEXICON

"Tipping point," the point at which new behaviors or new concepts move from resistance to acceptance.

In fact, it takes very little for a meme to tip into an epidemic. Malcolm Gladwell identifies only three elements for creating tipping points.[10] All are "small things."

1. The Few, the Proud, the Brave

Gladwell spotlights three types of community members who are most influential in creating tipping points: connectors, mavens, and salespersons. Only a few of each of these persons can ignite epidemics.

• *Connectors* are those rare few persons who have a gift for bringing the world together. They seem to know everyone and have the knack of making friends. Connectors are "people specialists" who collect acquaintances and provide social glue to groups. They create face-to-face epidemics and tipping points.

- *Mavens,* from a Yiddish word for people who accumulate knowledge, are information specialists. They simply know things the rest of us don't know. Mavens read more, observe better, ask quickly, and, most importantly, teach passionately. They are living data banks and information brokers who create word-of-mouth epidemics and tipping points.

- *Salespersons* are the persuaders and convincers who spur movements. They are likable, charming, energetic, exuberant, optimistic, and enthusiastic. Salespersons are gifted at "interactional synchrony," the ability to get "in-synch" with others easily and quickly. They sell heart-to-heart epidemics and tipping points.

2. The Stickiness Factor

Gladwell notes that the nature of the message itself creates momentum toward tipping points. Think about the *Sesame Street*™ strategy. Take one idea, repeat it over and over again, create experiences of discovery, wrap it all in story form–and you've moved toward stickiness through meaning and predictability.

3. The Power of Context

- Since behavior is often a function of place for people, when we change the context, we alter behavior. Changing little things over which we have control in our settings can make big differences. I was elected president of a service group and given the responsibility for shaping agendas for group meetings. To my surprise, some fairly subtle changes in agendas changed the flavor of the meetings radically.

- Since behavior is a function of people in places, when we create community, we create tipping points. Small, close-knit groups where beliefs are practiced and nurtured can increase change rates exponentially. Interestingly, the "rule of 150"–the number of people we can really know–provides one guideline for looking at community tipping points related to size.

Maintaining Momentum

When momentum and energy for ministry occurs, how can you maintain that precious impetus? Try these straightforward actions.

- *Simplify.* You know you've gotten to the gist of an idea when it's elegant in its simplicity. Stick to the basics.
- *Story-ize.* Wrap core messages inside stories. They become more concrete and memorable when people and plot lines carry the flow of the message's momentum.
- *Magnify success.* Build on momentum. As any physicist will quickly tell you, it's easier to keep a ball rolling than it is to get a ball rolling.

Epidemics in the Pews

Leading strategically is about creating grassroots epidemics in the pews of your church. Raise these clarifying questions for yourself.

- When can our whole church family be leavened with a "holy spirit"?
- How can our church become a more infectious community?
- Who are the people, what are the actions, and where are the times and places for epidemics to tip in our church?

Try this. Think of change as competition between multiple centers or among manifold forces of gravity vying with each other. Leaders link centers and network challengers. We grow communities of communities and coalitions of centers.

COACHING CONVERSATION

Congregational leaders usually lead multiple constituencies—unless they serve single-cell churches. Leaders become the hub for networks.[11] Or, they ally with one bloc and politicize their community for good or ill. Focusing within one center of gravity is complicated enough, but juggling an array of interests is truly a virtuoso act and may require a safety net.

✔ CASE STUDY: Matt Acts Strategically

Matt used family systems' thinking to understand why human groups rarely move forward in predictable fashion. His training in Freudian-based behavioral sciences had steeped him in the idea that behavior is controlled hydraulically by drives. Family systems showed him that there are more natural explanations for the way individuals and groups act. Matt knew how to focus his attention and how to keep an eye on the future. What he had never conquered was maintaining focus with flexibility. He gained a greater appreciation for the work of God's Spirit and for the tipping points of viral ideas.

Catch the Wave

The power of gravity and the persistence of tides are instructive for leaders who want to grow their strategic abilities. What are some of the lessons and applications we can learn from gravity and tides?

Strategy, When Applied to Community Life, Inevitably Has Highs and Lows

When the moon and sun align in what we call a new moon, their combined gravitational forces are exceptionally strong, creating very high and very low tides. We refer to these fluctuations as spring tides, even though the season has nothing to do with this phenomenon. Later, when the moon and sun aren't aligned, gravitational forces cancel each other out, and we get neap tides. Tides, by definition, ebb and flow.

COACHING CONVERSATION

Not all strategies work equally well. Some succeed, and others don't. Stay linked to the centering force of gravity rather than the bobbing waves.

Strategies Vary from Community to Community and Challenge to Challenge.

There are three kinds of tides.

1. Some parts of the world have one high and one low tide daily. Occurring in the northern Gulf of Mexico and Southeast Asia, these are called diurnal tides.
2. Semi-diurnal tides have two high and two low tides each day. These patterns are common to our Atlantic coasts and in Europe.
3. The west coasts of the United States and Canada have mixed tides, a variation of movements.

COACHING CONVERSATION

The flexibility of the leaders in Acts is a great reminder that we have to read situations, flow with new opportunities that appear before us, and tailor strategies to opportunities. The key is not to lose our basic focus.

Strategic Leaders Challenge Communities to Claim New Opportunities

Our country is hungry for electrical power. New underwater turbines[12] in the East River off New York City are now generating electric power by capturing the currents. These turbines turn at speeds slow enough that aquatic life isn't destroyed. It's a win-win solution that averts two crises—facing shortfalls of electrical power and upsetting ecological balance.

COACHING CONVERSATION

Brain research shows our primitive brains are geared to survival, while our more advanced brains solve problems. In other words, when in survival mode, we "fire" without saying "ready" or "aim." We react to the perceived threat. Leaders who can meet new opportunities calmly are as valuable as gold. When we maintain our calm, we can help our communities respond to challenges creatively, empowering our congregations to meet ministry futures.

Back to Basics

Leading strategically calls us to think about the basic organic leadership processes—connecting, centering, and challenging. Each of these processes can be a focus that requires flexibility and an eye for the future. Strategy is the most sophisticated cluster of actions any leader exercises.

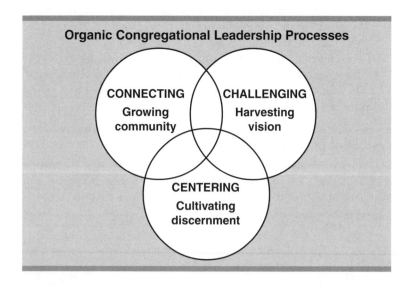

Organic Congregational Leadership Processes

CONNECTING
Growing
community

CHALLENGING
Harvesting
vision

CENTERING
Cultivating
discernment

Next Steps

Strategy and structure for leadership are rarely discussed in religious leadership. These explorations become much easier, however, when they are considered in an organic framework for ministry and leadership. Let's consider organic leader processes next.

CHAPTER 9

Planting Leadership Processes

Maybe Paul anticipated our day and our changing leadership challenges when he noted the "whole creation has been groaning as in the pains of childbirth" (Rom. 8:22). Something's being birthed in our world and in our faith communities. New expressions of "church" and "leadership" are emerging. But the seedbed for these new seeds is rocky because of our American traditions and assumptions.

How We Got This Way

Doctor Thornton, my college history professor, said, "History tells us how we got this way." Maybe a review of how American leaders got this way will help us see some of our psychic blind spots and then pave the way for us to try some new leader approaches and processes.

Historically, three root systems support American leadership.[1] These taproots have strongly impacted religious leadership, as well as the business scene:

1. Individualism versus teamwork
2. Competition versus cooperation
3. Authoritarianism versus participation

These stir the cauldron for American leaders. It's a doubly difficult mix for leaders of volunteer organizations. The tension of these opposites is frequently seen in the denominations growing from the Protestant Reformation.

Me versus Us

America began as the "New World," a wild frontier to be tamed by tough hands and hard heads. Immigrants, cut off from the "Old Country" and their extended families, came to make lives and fortunes on the frontier. Our earliest heroes were fearless explorers, military men, and industrialists who carved new beginnings from the wilderness with self-reliant, take-charge, competitive tactics. "Remember the Alamo!" shows us that even our failures were framed as moments of glory. This attitude cultivated individualistic leaders.

Alone versus Together

Our forefathers drafted three documents to safeguard the individual: the *Declaration of Independence,* the *Constitution,* and the *Bill of Rights.* Every single white male (at the time, remember, even this was revolutionary) had a vote, and every vote counted as much as any other vote. But America also emphasized majority rule. Individualism and cooperation remained–and still remain–in tension.

Bosses versus Teams

Immigrants brought the flavor of authoritarianism with them from Europe and Asia and introduced it into the American melting pot. As factories developed in industrializing America, the foremen became prototype commanders over their supervisees. Riding the tide of the Protestant work ethic, bosses squeezed productivity from their workers. One North Carolina textile tycoon, Moses Cone, built a Baptist and Methodist church adjacent to his mills. His motive was more commercial than religious. He had observed that his best foremen came from the lay leadership ranks of those two denominations.

The twentieth century brought individualism, cooperation, and authoritarianism together in the assembly lines, in an increasingly larger bureaucracy, and in the rise of the organization man. Even American media added their weight to the embedding of these values by interviewing and showcasing our industrial heroes. Our heritage produced a curious end result. While we preach teamwork, we idolize and reward individuals in America.

The Lone Ranger-type remains our prototypical hero–even in faith communities. It's part of our biblical tradition. The Old Testament prophet stood alone, drew lines in the sand, and claimed to speak with the authority of God. That lonely figure standing resolutely against the odds is a preferred image for religious leaders, particularly on the more conservative wing of American Protestantism. While the autocratic leader model suffered a bit from the falls of Jimmy Swaggart and Jim Bakker, it remained the most prevalent model both in American churches and in secular culture.

A Volatile Mix

In truth, trying to lead organizations of any kind–religious or secular–while using the mixture of individualism, cooperation, and authoritarianism has become increasingly less effective. With the rise of participative and human relations approaches in management, the loss of faith in many public and private institutions, and the arrival on the scene of post-scientific generations, the task of heroic leadership has gotten even weightier. Is it time for faith communities to live up to their ancient heritage and assume a counterculture stance again? Is it time to return to biblical approaches that fit our new era in history? That's exactly the possibility offered by organic leadership.

COACHING CONVERSATION

Given the American psyche's reliance on strength and power, Christ's servant example is always a distinctly minority stance in our culture. Leaders of faith communities are faced with a stark choice: our Christ or our culture. Do we believe Christ's church is alive? Are we willing to cultivate a more biblical approach for leading living churches? Do we need a "heart" transplant?

Organic Beliefs about Congregational Life Forces[2]

Leaders keep our communities heart-healthy. In sharp contrast to the organizations-as-machines view of the Industrial mind-set, organic leaders know our congregations are living entities and treat them accordingly. Organic thinking and leading is underpinned by a new set of old beliefs. These core assumptions provide a credo for organic leaders.

- In Christ's churches, God's Spirit brings health.
- We must carefully choose what we place in the active foreground of congregational life, because–for good or ill–it becomes our centering reality.

- Asking powerful questions frames our community's conversations and futures.
- We are more apt to move well into God's futures if we carry seeds of our healthiest pasts with us.
- Differences enrich us, and the ways we deal with differences reveal our views of God's kingdom.
- We must listen to our language carefully, since it tips off our inner vision, mental models, and core beliefs.
- Congregations are heliotropic and, revealingly, we follow our light and power source.
- Ministry priorities and actions show how practical and redemptive our community is.
- Congregations are living networks of living believers.
- Healthier communities and leaders who provide strong immune systems are our earthly hope for making Christ's kingdom come "on earth as it is in heaven" (Mt. 6:10).

COACHING CONVERSATION

Living things are led in distinct ways. We demonstrate our faith when we choose to lead by health and heart.

Process as Circulatory System

The human heart is a magical muscle. About the size of our fist and weighing in the range of nine to eleven ounces, it's an effective circulator of blood and oxygen for our bodies. It pumps more than 100,000 times each day, moving five quarts of blood through its chambers every minute. Our hearts are connected to 100,000 miles of pipelines to deliver blood to all parts of our bodies and to return it to our hearts for another voyage.

LEADER'S LEXICON

"Circulatory system," the array of organs and tissues that circulate blood and oxygen throughout our bodies, and, in this case, a metaphor for leadership processes.

The heart's effectiveness, in teamwork with other organs, is critical for human health and life. If blood ceases to circulate to our brain, permanent damage occurs within minutes. Our lungs are partners of the heart, too, removing carbon dioxide and refreshing the oxygen content. Our kidneys filter waste materials from our blood stream. These processes are quietly choreographed so that we only become aware of them when something goes wrong.

COACHING CONVERSATION

Think of the role of leadership as akin to our circulatory systems. Leadership moves unobtrusively to make the body of Christ live and breathe. Leaders energize every part of the community to keep it alive, healthy, and functioning.

The Flow of Processes

To advance a living kingdom of God, organic leaders lead by processes, flow, and natural growth. They plant and cultivate and feed and water, leaving the harvest to God. Leaders can take some cues from observing the flow of time. In earlier eras, before clocks and calendars were in every home or on every desk, time was apt to be measured by the king's reign. The ends of millennia, centuries, or even decades were rarely marked. Human beings have only observed the last five or six turns of century. Until then, the passage of time wasn't numbered as precisely as we try to mark it. Time just flowed forward and moved ahead.[3]

LEADER'S LEXICON

"Leadership Processes," the small cluster of basic leader actions—connecting, centering, and challenging—that keep congregations moving healthily.

For organic leaders, processes are channels in the flow and movement of maturing communities.[4] Healthy leadership processes have at least two qualities: credibility and openness. That is, they have integrity and a better than even chance of producing results. And, they bring and keep a variety of honest viewpoints in conversation.[5] Leaders of healthy processes constantly guide and nurture the flow of progress.

The Growth of Leaders

In our changing times and paradigms, leaders move, too. In fact, one key quality for process leaders is an immunity to motion sickness. They carry their comfort zones inside themselves and try to develop a high tolerance for ambiguity. Process leaders move forward in their thought forms and in their leadership patterns. Here are some of the most common contrasts and transitions between mechanical and organic approaches to leadership.

FROM→TO

Lines →Circles

Answers →Questions

Fixed Rules →Flexible Relationships

Levers →Links

"By-the-book" →"Go-with-the-flow"

Science →Art

Skills →Craft

How do you decide whether to help your community focus on connecting, centering, or challenging? Which organic leadership process do you bring into the foreground? The framework below will help you ask great questions, cultivate your intuition, and invest in the health of your community.

Organic Touchstones

Processes in leadership are straightforward to find and follow. Think in terms of five organic touchstones.

1. Find the health–those pools of energy at work in your congre-gation–and feed them.
2. Match one of the basic organic leadership actions–connecting, centering, or challenging–to the energy at the heart of your community and bring that leadership action into the foreground of your community's life.
3. Begin where there's the most energy and see that process through.
4. Use questions to shape the agenda.
5. When the focal process has run its course, follow a strategic mental map by moving on to the next energy pool that's emerging.

Leaders are catalysts for movement toward health and courageous ministry in faith communities. But, hang on for a bumpy ride. Folks have been caught in the mechanistic rut for so long any change will seem like a jolt or even a betrayal.

A-C-T-S Is More Than a New Testament Book

We've identified three basic leader processes—connecting, centering, and challenging. These three ongoing, overlapping actions provide the steering currents for congregational life and ministry. However, there is a preliminary, behind-the-scenes kind of "radar" that helps leaders act with confidence.

Adopting new leadership behaviors is always a stretch. Maybe a memory aid will help make this more covert scanning framework memorable and portable for you. Use A-C-T-S to help you think of leadership as an organic process.

- *A=Assess*, or Flowing with the "Go"

    (Where and when is our community most lively?)

- *C=Coach*, or Clarifying the Core

    (How do we focus our community for action?)

- *T=Trigger*, or Moving the Mood

    (How can we move the emotional direction of our community?)

- *S=Sense-Make*, or Finding the Frames

    (How can we interpret reality and create memories for our community?)

"Assessing" Processes Help Leaders "Flow with the 'Go'"

Conventional wisdom is more apt to encourage us to "go with the flow," but that advice doesn't provide a useful diagnostic filter for leaders. As a beginning point, organic leaders look for the "go," the pools of energy in the faith community. Look for the signs of health and vitality to build on. It's easier to make a healthy community even healthier than to make a sick one well.

Here's an illustration of "flowing with the 'go'." In collaborative projects, leaders are well advised to begin with community building rather than common issues. Otherwise, groups tend to fragment around advocating for interests instead of gathering around community. We can begin with some knowledge of others' stories. When community happens, it gives us an identity, a sense of belonging, a measure of security, and some mutual hopes. Meaning and memory flow together. We become people with a common story.[6]

Leadership shared is leadership squared. In John Kotter's words, collaborative leadership is spelled with a little, lower case "*l.*"[7] While not as flashy or attention-grabbing as Industrial models, organic leaders grow relationships, help vision emerge, and move with the community toward action.

Within communities, Peter Drucker points leaders toward working with "islands of health and strength."[8] The energy of health shows you where the motivation is at the moment. What psychology calls motivation, this inner reservoir of energy, is a precious clue to the soul of your community. Theologically speaking, the "go" is God's Spirit at work in your group. When you discover where the "go" is, you become a steward of God's empowerment of your community. Don't squander the "go." That's the point. Find the "go," and then flow with it to see it flourish for harvest.

Clue questions for discovering the "go" include:

- What's positive with our community now?
- What's our community ready to plan now?
- What's our community primed to do now?
- Where's the energy pooling in our community now?
- Where's the most joy, laughter, and fun in our community now?
- Where's the most fire, passion, heart, and heat in our community now?
- Where's the most health and vitality in our community now?
- Is our faith community more primed to trust or discern or risk right now?

When we have identified the projects, issues, and ministries our community is called to, we've found the "go." With that discovery, our next question is: "Does this energy relate primarily to connecting or centering or challenging?" The answer to that question points to where we put our energy. We become stewards of our communities' energy to move us more deeply into the basic organic leadership process where we can make the most immediate investment.

Sports and games show us the power of momentum or flow. When it occurs, it's virtually unstoppable. Consider energy and momentum a gift of God's Spirit. Cultivate it. Steward it well.

"Coaching" Processes Help Leaders "Clarify the Core"

When we coach fellow community leaders and others to find and follow their passions, we're enabling them to clarify their core beliefs. Centered communities and centered leaders recognize, rely on, and rally around their core convictions. Look at the *G-O-A-L-S* acronym and its core movements to help persons identify and pursue their goals.

- *G*raphing Pathways–from here to where?
- *O*ptimizing Possibilities–this or that?
- *A*cting for Progress–from here to there!
- *L*imiting Paralysis–up and over!
- *S*upporting Passages–on and on!

Using the image of an athletic coach, Ron Richardson, family systems' expert, describes the perspective of relating as a pastoral coach to members inside congregations:

> Good coaches are well connected to their teams and know the strengths and liabilities of their players. They are interested in the lives of their players, not just their athletic skills. They can see the bigger picture. They look at the field from the wide-angle, more distant perspective. They also know the playbook. They have studied the dynamics of the game and the moves of the opposing team. They have a sense of the whole as well as the individual parts.[9]

Leaders who coach communities systemically help members find their core beliefs while in motion. Coaching helps other leaders and entire communities "get to the heart of the matter." Press these core questions:

- What are you hungry to do now?
- Are you ready to act now?

• Other than encouragement before the fact and accountability after the fact, what do you need from me now?

COACHING CONVERSATION

What's your calling? What are your gifts? Where's your passion? What's your heart hungry for now? How can you pursue your goals now? When leaders can help their communities answer these questions with clarity and confidence, they have unleashed a powerful force.

"Triggering" Processes Help Leaders "Move the Mood"

This action is largely an invisible leadership action exercised mostly by "touch." When we trigger our communities to move from one action or project to another, we "move the mood." Part of knowing when and how to trigger a group is intuition, part is analytical, and none of it is "in the books."

Let me offer a specific scenario for you. Imagine a work team meeting. Your group is working through its agenda point-by-point. Then, the group begins to wander emotionally and lose its way. You can feel and see the restlessness and lack of focus. The odds are high that a "trigger" has been missed. When your group focuses on an agenda item and finishes it, exercise timing and trigger the group forward. It may be as easy as asking, "Anything else related to this item? No? Good work. Now, let's move to the next item on our agenda." Watch what happens to the energy in the room. Most of the time, you'll feel the group relax, gather its emotional energy, and move ahead with new momentum and fresh intentionality.

To help you trigger your group, ask yourself these questions:

• Am I keeping the community's energy focused on one-issue-at-a-time?

• Am I anticipating the next "flow" in the process?

• Am I considering options for whatever comes after whatever's next?

• Am I monitoring energy levels and mood swings?

• Am I ready to refocus energy by triggering the community to move to a new issue, action, or project?

"Sense-making" Processes Help Leaders "Find the Frames"[10]

Leaders sense the silent hopes of their communities and put those yearnings into public words for their groups. They "frame" the message or vision with the same effect that a picture frame has when it limits a favorite photograph. Frames enrich visions, cross-pollinating ideas across categories and awakening memories. Framed messages take otherwise abstract issues, create mental models of them, turn challenges into positive options, add focus and concreteness to them, and prime communities for action.

Leaders are sense-makers. They look for stories and pictures of hope and health in the system, those life-signaling "possibility conversations."[11] They create "common sense," or sense in community. "Sense" multiplies our impact by helping define meaning and by creating memories. Meaning explains new realities for us, and memories revive old realities for us.

To guide sense-making, leaders ask themselves:

- Which stories, metaphors, and mental models "make sense" in this situation for me? for us?
- Which experiences or patterns of meaning "make memories" in this situation for me? for us?
- When does energy pool in my community?
- How is God's will framed within my community for me and for us?

An Old Testament story illustrates framing for us. Remember when David visited his brothers and heard Goliath's dare to them. The Hebrew soldiers were saying: "He's so big we'll never beat him!" However, David reframed the situation and gave himself permission to take the dare. He said to himself: "He's so big, I can't miss him!" That's Framing 101 for leaders.

Frame-finding builds on the leader's own sense of self and soul. When leaders demonstrate a calm, centered leadership stance, the community can face its realities and possibilities with more faith and less anxiety.

Anxiety and Leader Processes

Anxiety and leadership are an odd couple; they go together but may work against each other. Note these contrasts. Anxiety is nature's early-warning, high-alert system. It's message: Act now for self-preservation! Leadership weaves the community's tapestry of connecting, centering, and challenging processes. It's message: Act now for health! Anxiety is a primitive reaction for human survival. Leadership is an immune response to keep communities healthy. It's far too easy for these forces to counterbalance or to cancel each other out. Leaders make the difference and, through immunity, tilt the balance toward health.

Two particular expressions of anxiety are special competitors for leaders: anxiety's contagion path and anxiety's binders.[12]

1. Anxiety spreads like waves radiating out from a pebble thrown into a pond.

One anxious "carrier" can infect an entire community. The first wave for the carrier's dis-ease is the "caregiver" who's most emotionally sensitized to the carrier. Then, attempting to make the carrier happy, the caregiver gives the lead to the most anxious and reactive members of the community as they work to pacify the carrier. It's like the old saying, "The patients are in charge of the asylum." Communities without clear centers or strongly immune leaders are most susceptible to being immobilized by runaway anxiety.

2. Anxiety multiplies itself more easily in certain community situations.

Some issues are especially potent binders for anxiety. Success and achievement are good anxiety binders. Beliefs are even stronger anxiety binders. Relationships are the most powerful anxiety binders of them all. Each of these slices of life—contribution, conviction, and community—is pivotal in congregational life. Blend them together, and they make leadership in faith communities a real maze.

When anxiety spikes, communities tend to get bossier and more authoritarian, more helpless and dependent, more edgy and irritated, or more intolerant and more narrow-minded. Or, in some cases, they do all of the above. Problem-solving ability and creativity plummet during high-anxiety episodes. The primitive brain kicks in and produces some less than stellar brainstorms. Note some bad problem-solving options:

Either!/Or! Thinking
"Always" and "Never" Language
!!!The-Sky-Is-Falling Reactions!!!
First Idea = Best Idea
Where's the Magic Bullet to Rescue Us?
I Can't Find the Real Me!
Give Me Any Triangle or Ally–Now!

Predictably, communities fall into blaming, resisting, reorganizing, self-protecting, losing creativity, and working heroically in an effort to deal with their discontent. In the end, only increasing health and immunity will dampen anxiety and its corrosive effects.

COACHING CONVERSATION

Anxiety corrodes health. But, leaders give hope. Invest yourself in dampening anxiety and raising immunity.

Organic Leadership Processes

Churches are living communities and require organic leadership, but where do organic leaders focus their leadership conversations?

1. Connecting Conversations: Leaders need the company of others who relate to them because they hold values in common with each other. Scripture reminds us that the basic human hunger to relate to others goes back to creation itself: "The LORD God said, 'It is not good for man to be alone.'" (Gen. 2:18).

The giant redwoods, so large and so tall that winds can topple them, stabilize themselves by interweaving their root systems with the trees around them. They literally hold each other up. Leaders strengthen root systems for mutual support and nourishment. Their communities help them balance "me" needs and "we" needs healthily.

2. Centering Conversations: Leaders need a sense of depth in their groups, a set of core beliefs. Centering their communities in discerning God's will provides them with a basic pull of gravity that centers them healthily.

3. Challenging Conversations: Leaders need a future together with their communities. Vision impacts leaders *and* communities. As

the Sage noted, "Where there is no vision, the people perish" (Prov. 29:18, KJV). Challenging the community to harvest its vision is the health plan of organic leaders. The steering current of vision shapes future directions.

Process Leadership—Inside/Outside

Throughout this book, especially in the treatments of connecting, centering, and challenging, I've emphasized the balance between personal growth and congregational leadership. Let me return to that theme again and point out the personal dimensions of the three basic leader processes.

Theology often speaks of the triad of love, faith, and hope. Each of these qualities is a theme for leader growth. Note the model below:

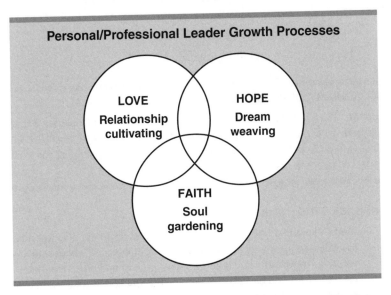

Personally and theologically speaking, love is the **seedbed for connecting** and raises key questions about cultivating relationships.

- How can I be a trustworthy family member?
- How can I become a tried and true friend?
- How can I remain a loyal mate?
- How can I become a dependable parent?
- How can I serve as a faithful church leader?

Personally and theologically speaking, faith is the **seedbed for centering** and raises key questions about soul gardening.

- How can I deepen my spiritual life?
- How can I stay open to God's surprises?
- How can I keep routine spiritual disciplines fresh?
- How can I make room for new insights into faith and life?
- How can I find my best discovery channels to God?

Personally and theologically speaking, hope is the **seedbed for challenging** and raises key questions about dream weaving.

- How can I hear the call of God clearly?
- How can I discover and use my core ministry gifts?
- How can I use my best leadership strengths?
- How can I frame my future?
- How can I live on God's horizons?

COACHING CONVERSATION

Leadership is always a two-sided coin—personal and professional. Some leaders concentrate on personal development and become ingrown. Others invest in professional growth and lose their souls. Both sides of the coin are valuable and necessary.

✔ CASE STUDY: Matt's Key Processes

Matt's exploration of family systems reduced his leadership agenda. He watched for triangles. He focused on getting clear about what he valued as a leader. He worked at staying calm and clear. He tried to challenge the status quo. At heart, Matt functioned as a source of immunity for his congregation. Define, regulate, and challenge. Those simple actions guided Matt's practice of organic leadership.

Signposts for the Journey

Recently I was on the Blue Ridge Parkway and saw a sign at one of the rare rest areas: "Last gasoline for 50 miles." It was a sober reminder to fuel up before it's too late. That's always a fair warning. So here's a final reminder about the primary model for organic leadership. Read it carefully. You may not see it again for a long while.

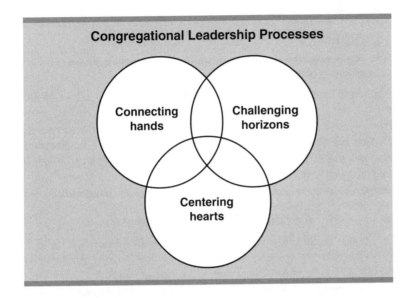

Congregational Leadership Processes

Connecting hands

Challenging horizons

Centering hearts

Planting Leadership Seeds in Our Own Lives

Most of us are naturally more gifted at some things than we are at others. Are you more comfortable with connecting, centering, or challenging? Take a moment and rank these three leader initiatives in the order of their comfort levels for you. What's your ranking?

In general, leaders try to see clearly. But sometimes they're blind anyway. Here are some potential lessons from that simple ranking to help you confront two kinds of blindness.

- You may take your greatest strength for granted and be oblivious of it. That's the *blindness of giftedness*. In the sports world, great natural athletes are often poor teachers. What they do by instinct is difficult or impossible for them to translate and demonstrate deliberately.

- You may avoid your greatest weakness and leave yourself vulnerable. That's the *blindness of avoidance*. In any community, all three leadership processes are needed for effectiveness, balance, and health.

You may want to consider two ways to deal with the potential blind spots of your weakness:

1. Be sure the community's leadership team can initiate all three processes.

2. Cultivate your weaknesses enough to help you appreciate their importance to community life.

COACHING CONVERSATION

Appreciate your gifts and use them well. Know your weaknesses and keep them from sabotaging you and your community. Grow, grow, grow. Remember the old joke about the way to get to Carnegie Hall? "Practice, practice, practice." That advice also applies to growing yourself as an organic leader in the kingdom of God. So, go and plant, cultivate, and harvest— beginning with yourself.

You Can Practice Organic Leadership

You already know how to practice organic leadership, even if you've not been encouraged to think and act organically. You've been a child, a friend, maybe a parent, a pet owner, a plant grower, or a team member. You've already begun the journey. Keep on going.

Traveling Mercies

May God bless our journey as lively leaders for living churches. May God give us traveling mercies.

One Final Coaching Conversation

Thanks for joining me in an exploration of *Seeds for the Future*. We have just enough time left for one final coaching conversation about the web of organic leadership ideas. For review, let me repeat and highlight them again for you once more.

1. *Organic leaders sow and grow.*
   At the most basic level leaders focus on sowing lots of ministry ideas and growing lots of new leaders for the future.
2. *Leaders are clear about why they're here.*
   Discover your deepest calling. Grow yourself more deeply into that passion and strength.
3. *Living organisms are led differently than machines.*
   If you're convinced the church of Jesus Christ is alive, lead organically. Learn organic approaches from God's creation.
4. *Living things change.*
   Organic leaders count on God to create change and are willing to live on God's change schedule. Sometimes we race to catch up. Sometimes we wait on the fullness of time. In either case, we remain patient and calm.
5. *Without a community, there are no leaders.*
   Organic leaders grow relationships. They get connected to the community and stay connected. They cultivate connections and nurture them over time.

6. *Centered communities have depth.*
   Organic leaders find their center. They define who they are, what they believe, and what they stand for.
7. *Without courage, vision is dead on arrival.*
   Challenging our faith systems to change calls for healthier and more immune communities. It takes courage to stand for a vision.
8. *Living things self-organize into flexible but stable structures.*
   Organic leaders appreciate both flexibility and stability. They count on creation to mentor them in structures.
9. *Organic leaders focus with flexibility on the future.*
   A multiple-choice world calls us to choose "which." Limited resources push us to decide "when." Those are the strategic issues for organic leaders.
10. *Leaders keep their communities heart healthy.*
   Processes keep organic leaders in the heart of their communities' energy flow. They grow themselves in order to lead others.

Seeds for Our Future

You as an organic leader have at least ten seeds for the future. A seed has only one purpose in creation—to germinate and grow. But a seed is only potential until it's planted, protected, nourished, and nurtured. It's a miniature time capsule for its parent plant, preserving DNA and holding heritage and future. When we plant a seed, we invest our lives in the future. So let me encourage you to sow freely. "Whoever sows sparingly will also reap sparingly, and whoever sows generously will also reap generously" (2 Cor. 9:6).

- Plant the seeds.
- Cultivate the seeds.
- Harvest the seeds.

Leaders focus on three ongoing, overlapping, and complementary processes: connecting, centering, and challenging. They seed communities, weaving webs of relationships and cultivating trust. They seed centers, encouraging spiritual growth and discerning God's will. They seed challenge, stirring communities to leave comfort zones behind and to grow toward health. Organic leaders plant seeds with calm patience and gentleness.

A Prayer for the Journey

"Nothing is so strong as gentleness. Nothing is so gentle as strength," observed Frances de Sales, bishop of Geneva in the seventeenth century.

Don't lose any opportunity, however small, of being gentle toward everyone.

Don't rely on your own efforts to succeed in your various undertakings, but only on God's help.

Then rest in God's care of you, confident that he will do what is best for you provided that you will, for your part, work diligently but gently.

I say "gently" because a tense diligence is harmful both to your heart and to your task and is not real diligence, but rather over-eagerness and anxiety.

I recommend you to God's mercy.

I beg God, through that same mercy, to fill you with his love.

NOTES

Part 1: Cultivating Sowers, Seeds, and Seasons

[1]A. M. Hunter, *Gleanings from the New Testament* (Philadelphia: Westminster Press, 1975), 56–59.

[2]Daniel A. Tagliere, *People, Power, and Organization* (New York: AMACOM, 1973).

Chapter 1: Growing Self, Growing Soul

[1]Terry Hershey, *Soul Gardening* (Minneapolis: Augsburg Fortress Press, 2002).

[2]Robert Fulghum, *It Was on Fire When I Lay Down on It* (New York: Villard Books, 1989), 70.

[3]Frederick Buechner, cited in *Horizons: Theologian Notes Impact of FTE Fellowship* 8, no. 1 (Winter 2005): 1.

[4]Warren Bennis, *On Becoming a Leader* (Reading, Mass.: Addison-Wesley, 1989), 3.

[5]Paula Bernstein, *Family Ties, Corporate Bonds* (Garden City, N.Y.: Doubleday, 1985).

[6]Emotional process is a fundamental theme of Bowen family systems theory and explores multigenerational transmission of behavior patterns and blind spots. For more information on this issue, see Murray Bowen, *Family Therapy in Clinical Practice* (New York: Aronson, 2002) and Michael E. Kerr and Murray Bowen, *Family Evaluation* (New York: W. W. Norton, 1988).

[7]Memes are viral ideas that shape cultures and are similar to genes in individuals. For a treatment of memes, including a perspective on memes in Christianity, see Aaron Lynch, *Thought Contagion: How Belief Spreads through Society* (New York: Basic Books, 1996).

[8]For an interesting research study demonstrating that leaders who have revolutionized both science and religion have primarily been "laterborns," see Frank J. Sulloway, *Born to Rebel: Birth Order, Family Dynamics, and Creative Lives* (New York: Pantheon, 1996).

[9]For the best resource on exploring and understanding your own family system, see Ronald W. Richardson, *Becoming a Healthier Pastor: Family Systems Theory and the Pastor's Own Family* (Minneapolis: Fortress Press, 2005).

[10]Three books that inform the broader processes of mentoring and being mentored are Bob Buford, *Halftime: Changing Your Game Plan from Success to Significance* (Grand Rapids, Mich.: Zondervan, 1994); Zalman Schachter-Shalomi, *From Aging to Sage-ing: A Profound Vision of Growing Older* (New York: Warner Books, 1995); and Joseph L. Badaracco Jr., *Defining Moments: When Managers Must Choose between Right and Right* (Boston: Harvard Business School, 1997).

[11]Mac preached a sermon from John 10:10 on the abundant life. He used the homely analogy that mashed potatoes, when seasoned with salt, pepper, and butter, take on abundant flavor. I've never forgotten that description.

[12]Sheldon's original book is out of print, but his younger relative has written a helpful update. See Garrett W. Sheldon and Deborah Morris, *What Would Jesus Do?* (Nashville: Broadman and Holman, 1998).

[13]See Daniel Goleman, *Emotional Intelligence: Why It Can Matter More Than IQ* (New York: Bantam, 1995) and *Working with Emotional Intelligence* (New York: Bantam, 1998); and Daniel Goleman, Annie McKee, and Richard E. Boyatzis, *Primal Leadership: Realizing the Power of Emotional Intelligence* (Boston: Harvard Business School, 2002). For a more technical treatment of emotional intelligence, see Reuven Bar-On and James D. A. Parker, eds., *The Handbook of Emotional Intelligence: Theory, Development, Assessment, and Application at Home, School, and in the Workplace* (San Francisco: Jossey-Bass, 2000).

[14]For insights into how artisans develop strategic thinking abilities, see Henry Mintzberg, "Crafting Strategy," *Harvard Business Review*, Reprint No. 87407 (1987), Harvard Business School Publishing Division, Boston, Mass. 02163.

[15]Henri J.M. Nouwen, *The Return of the Prodigal Son* (New York: Image/Doubleday, 1992). Jürgen Moltmann and Elisabeth Moltmann-Wendel's *Passion for God: Theology in Two Voices* (Louisville: Westminster John Knox Press, 2003), 57–67, has a wonderful exploration of Jesus' prayer in Gethsemane. Discipleship is another basic theme that's explored by Douglas D. Webster in *The Discipline of Surrender: Biblical Images of Discipleship* (Downers Grove, Ill.: InterVarsity Press, 2001).

[16]Jim Cymbala's books, *Fresh Wind, Fresh Fire* (Grand Rapids, Mich.: Zondervan, 1997) and *Fresh Faith* (Grand Rapids, Mich.: Zondervan, 1999), are helpful recent accounts of a congregation responding to the Holy Spirit.

[17]Reading classics such as Thomas à Kempis's *The Imitation of Christ*, first printed in Latin in 1471, is a common and helpful practice.

[18]Reuben Job has compiled a forty-day process of readings and prayers called *A Guide to Spiritual Discernment* (Nashville: Upper Room, 1996).

[19]An option for identifying theological and ministry themes for moviegoers is suggested by Adele Reinhartz's *Scripture on the Silver Screen* (Louisville: Westminster John Knox Press, 2003).

[20]Phillip Gulley's *Home Town Tales* (Sisters, Oreg.: Multnomah, 1998); Jeff Berryman's *Leaving Ruin* (Orange, Calif.: New Leaf Books, 2002) and J. Philip Wogaman's *An Unexpected Journey: Reflections on Pastoral Ministry* (Louisville: Westminster John Knox Press, 2004) are examples of fictional and biographical materials that instruct.

[21]Ramesh Richard, *Mending Your Soul: The Spiritual Path to Wholeness* (Nashville: Broadman and Holman, 1999).

[22]Perspective is critical for leaders. In the early days of mapmaking, long before satellite imagery literally gave us the "big picture," bias was common in cartography. Typically, the center of the universe was wherever the mapmaker was. And that center was often depicted in larger-than-life-and-reality images. Leaders, especially religious leaders, can learn from this cautionary tale of warped perspective. See J. B. Hartley, *The New Nature of Maps: Essays in the History of Cartography* (Baltimore: Johns Hopkins University, 2001).

[23]Danny E. Morris and Charles M. Olsen, *Discerning God's Will Together: A Spiritual Practice for the Church* (Nashville: Upper Room, 1997), 58–59.

[24]Some corporate boards prefer combat veterans as CEOs because military leaders have been severely tested, don't rattle easily, understand sacrificing to do the right thing, have made life-or-death decisions in the face of uncertainty, learn from immediate feedback, develop care for colleagues, and know how to lead and to follow. Persons with combat as a shaping experience are rarer now than at any time since the beginning of the Industrial Revolution. See Del Jones, "A Vanishing Breed: CEOs Seasoned by Military Combat," *USA Today*, 19 January 2005, B1–2.

[25]Warren G. Bennis and Robert Thomas, in *Geeks and Geezers: Leading and Learning for a Lifetime* (Boston: Harvard Business School, 2002), have produced a fascinating study of how eras, values, and defining moments shape leaders. They compare the World Wars and the Great Depression to the dot-com collapse and "fractured families" and wonder if today's leaders have had the crucible experiences to forge them for high-quality leadership.

[26]Richard Lischer, *Open Secrets: A Spiritual Journey through a Country Church* (New York: Doubleday, 2001), 76–77.

[27]See Daniel J. Levinson, et al., *The Seasons of a Man's Life* (New York: Alfred A. Knopf, 1978) and *The Seasons of a Woman's Life* (New York: Alfred A. Knopf, 1996) for ways life, career, and leadership are formed in early adult life.

[28]Robert D. Dale, *Leading Edge: Leadership Strategies from the New Testament* (Nashville: Abingdon Press, 1996), 105–15.

[29]Dan P. McAdams's *Stories We Live By: Personal Myths and the Making of the Self* (New York: William Morrow, 1993) stresses that we shape our life stories and generally reflect either optimistic or pessimistic outlooks.

Chapter 2: Your Church Is Alive

[1]Rolf Jensen, *The Dream Society* (New York: McGraw-Hill, 1999).

[2]Barry Oshry, *Seeing Systems: Unlocking the Mysteries of Organizational Life* (San Francisco: Berrett-Koehler, 1995), 4.

[3]Thomas Hine, "Looking Alive," *The Atlantic Monthly* (November 2001): 120.

[4]Peter M. Senge, "Leadership in Living Organizations," in *The Leader of the Future: New Visions, Strategies, and Practices for the Next Era,* ed. Frances Hesselbein, Marshall Goldstein, and Richard Beckhard (San Francisco: Jossey-Bass, 1996), 74.

[5]Oshry, *Seeing Systems,* 1.

[6]Paula Bernstein, *Family Ties, Corporate Bonds* (Garden City, N.J.: Doubleday, 1985).

[7]Oshry, *Seeing Systems,* 13.

[8] Senge, "Leadership in Living Organizations," 77.

[9]Margaret J. Wheatley, *Leadership and the New Science: Discovering Order in a Chaotic World,* 2d. ed. (San Francisco: Berrett-Koehler, 1999), xi.

[10]Christian A. Schwarz, *Paradigm Shift in the Church: How Natural Church Development Can Transform Theological Thinking* (Carol Stream, Ill.: ChurchSmart Resources, 1999), 233–51. Schwarz describes church growth in "biotic" terms, or as "autopoiesis." He identifies six biotic principles that are involved in the growth of living things: interdependence, multiplication, energy transformation, multi-usage, symbiosis, and functionality.

[11]Peter L. Steinke, *Healthy Congregations: A Systems Approach* (Washington, D.C.: Alban Institute, 1996), 91.

[12]For an interesting perspective on multigenerational immunocompetence, see Jennifer L. Grindstaff, Edmund D. Brodie III, and Ellen D. Ketterson, "Immune Function across Generations," Proceedings of The Royal Society (2003), 270: 2309–2319.

[13]Self-care is critical, but methods are often debated. Satchel Paige, the legendary baseball pitcher, had some quirky ideas about calming oneself and managing diet. Among other things, he counseled, "Avoid fried foods which angry up the blood," and, "If your stomach disputes you, lie down and pacify it." See Mike McGovern's *The Complete Idiot's Guide to Sports History and Trivia* (New York: Alpha Books, 2001), 42.

[14]Norman Cousins, *Anatomy of an Illness as Perceived by the Patient* (New York: W. W. Norton, 1979). This anecdotal report is a "been there, done that" testimony of the power of faith, hope, love, courage, and laughter to stimulate healing.

[15]"Autoimmunity," *QPB Science Encyclopedia* (New York: Helicon, 1998), 65.

Chapter 3: Already in Progress

[1]Janine M. Benyus, *Biomimicry: Innovation by Nature* (Perennial: New York, 1997).

[2]Margaret J. Wheatley, *Leadership and the New Science: Discovering Order in a Chaotic World,* 2d ed. (San Francisco: Berrett-Koehler, 1999), 18.

[3]Gerhard Von Rad, *Genesis: A Commentary,* The Old Testament Library (Philadelphia: Westminster Press, 1961), 220.

[4]Wheatley, *Leadership and the New Science,* 21.

[5]Thomas F. Farrell, II, "Law Helps Consumers during Transition," *Richmond (VA) Times-Dispatch,* 22 February 2004, E1.

[6]Bernd Heinrich, *Winter World: The Ingenuity of Animal Survival* (New York: HarperCollins, 2003), 41.

[7]Ibid., 29.

[8]Bucky McMahon, "The Living Machines," *Esquire* (December 2004): 214–19.

[9]Deepak Chopra, *The New Physics of Healing* audiocassette (Boulder, Colo.: Sounds True Recordings).

[10]Benyus, *Biomimicry,* 11–58.

[11]Lisa Lucio Gough, "Neighbors Helping Milky Way Grow," *Richmond (VA) Times-Dispatch,* 2 October 2003, F3.

[12]Michael Schrage, *Serious Play* (Boston: Harvard Business School, 2000), 27–29.

[13]The image of change's cascades in Bob Wall, Robert S. Solum, Mark B. Sobol, *The Visionary Leader* (Rocklin, Calif.: Prima, 1992) is a powerful organic notion.

[14]William Bridges, *Transitions* (Reading, Mass.: Addison-Wesley, 1980). I've revised Bridges's transitions model, especially in the middle phase I've called "turnings." The concept of "turning" is borrowed from and based on Emilie Griffin's *Turning: Reflections on the Experience of Conversion* (Garden City, N.Y.: Doubleday, 1980).

[15]Beth Ann Gaede, ed., *Ending with Hope* (Washington, D.C.: Alban Institute, 2002).

[16]See Wheatley, *Leadership and the New Science,* 115–34. This material introduces readers to "chaos and the strange attractor of meaning."

[17]Ibid., 22–23.

[18]Readers who are familiar with systemic views of leadership, especially those drawn from the family systems theory of Murray Bowen, will recognize the root system for most of the leadership processes described here. These processes are framed in terms of congregational leadership more than therapeutic actions. See Murray Bowen, *Family Therapy in Clinical Practice* (Northvale, N.J.: Aronson, 2002); Michael E. Kerr and Murray Bowen, *Family Evaluation: An Approach Based on Bowen Theory* (New York: W. W. Norton, 1988); Edwin Friedman, *Generation to Generation* (New York: Guilford, 1985); Patricia A. Comella, Joyce Bader, Judith S. Ball, Kathleen K. Wiseman, and Ruth Riley Sagar, eds., *The Emotional Side of Organizations: Applications of Bowen Theory* (Washington, D.C.: Georgetown Family Center, 1996); Ronald W. Richardson, *Creating a Healthier Church: Family Systems Theory, Leadership, and Congregational Life* (Minneapolis: Fortress Press, 1996); Peter L. Steinke, *Healthy Congregations: A Systems Approach* (Washington, D.C.: Alban Institute, 1996); and Mary Beth O'Neill, *Executive Coaching with Backbone and Heart: A Systems Approach to Engaging Leaders with Their Challenges* (San Francisco: Jossey-Bass, 2000).

[19]O'Neill, *Executive Coaching,* 83–86.

[20]James Surowiecki, *The Wisdom of Crowds: Why the Many Are Smarter Than the Few and How Collective Wisdom Shapes Business, Economics, Societies, and Nations* (New York: Random House, 2004).

[21]Howard Gardner, *Changing Minds* (Boston: Harvard Business School Press, 2004), 69. Gardner points out that democratic communities share power: "In a democracy, an elected leader has power, but little of it is there for the taking."

Chapter 4: Connecting 101

[1]In some groups, "viewshed" is also used to refer to the sight vistas in scenic areas.

[2]For a fuller conversation about the "we-with" theme, see Robert D. Dale, *Sharing Ministry with Volunteer Leaders* (Nashville: Convention Press, 1986), 56–68.

[3]"Parasite," *QPB Science Encyclopedia* (New York: Helicon, 1998), 555.

[4]"Comensalism," *QPB Science Encyclopedia,* 177.

[5]"Mutualism," *QPB Science Encyclopedia,* 508.

[6]Charles Culbertson, "Statler Brother Captures Sense of Community," *Richmond (VA) Times-Dispatch,* 29 August 2004, E4.

[7]David J. Wood, "Let's Meet," *Christian Century* (February 10, 2004): 24–29.

[8]Robert D. Putnam, "Bowling Alone: America's Declining Social Capital," *Journal of Democracy* 6:1 (January 1995): 65–78.

[9]Ellen Berscheid and Elaine Hatfield Walster, *Interpersonal Attraction,* 2d ed. (Reading, Mass.: Addison-Wesley, 1978).

[10]Malcolm Gladwell, *The Tipping Point: How Little Things Can Make a Big Difference* (Boston: Brown, Little and Company, 2000), 30–88.

[11]Erik H. Erikson, "Identity and the Life Cycle," *Psychological Issues* 1, no. 1 (New York: International Universities Press, 1959).

[12]William Zinsser, *Writing about Your Life: A Journey into the Past* (New York: Marlowe and Company, 2004), 182.

[13]Ibid., 22.

[14]Robert Bruce Shaw, *Trust in the Balance: Building Successful Organizations on Results, Integrity, and Concern* (San Francisco: Jossey-Bass, 1997).

[15]James M. Kouzes and Barry Z. Posner, *Encouraging the Heart: A Leader's Guide to Rewarding and Recognizing Others* (San Francisco: Jossey-Bass, 1998).

[16]For an online description of this research and its findings, see Thom S. Rainer, "Leaders Admit Top 5 Weaknesses," http//www.churchcentral.com/nw/s/template/Article.html/id/21459.

[17]James M. Kouzes and Barry Z. Posner, *Credibility: How Leaders Gain and Lose It, Why People Demand It* (San Francisco: Jossey-Bass, 1993).

[18]James Burke, *The Pinball Effect: How Renaissance Water Gardens Made the Carburetor Possible—and Other Journeys through Knowledge* (Boston: Little, Brown and Company, 1996), 5.

Chapter 5: Centering 101

[1]Donald O. Clifton and Paula Nelson, *Soar with Your Strengths* (New York: Dell, 1996).

[2]These questions flow out of the research and writing of two primary sources. The issues for the first three life stages are identified primarily in Daniel J. Levinson's classic study *The Seasons of a Man's Life* (New York: Knopf, 1978), and the final stage is explored specifically in Richard J. Leider and David A. Shapiro, *Claiming Your Place at the Fire: Living the Second Half of Your Life on Purpose* (San Francisco: Berrett-Kohler, 2004). Enriching the perspective to these questions are the additional resources of Daniel J. Levinson with Judy D. Levinson, *The Seasons of a Woman's Life* (New York: Knopf, 1996) and Frederic M. Hudson, *The Adult Years: Mastering the Art of Self-Renewal* (San Francisco: Jossey-Bass, 1991).

[3]Bob Buford, *Half Time: Changing Your Game Plan from Success to Significance* (Grand Rapids, Mich.: Zondervan, 1994).

[4]Bob Buford, *Finishing Well: What People Who Really Live Do Differently!* (Nashville: Integrity Publishers, 2004).

[5]L. H. Marshall, *The Challenge of New Testament Ethics* (London: Macmillan, 1947), 60–62.

[6]Danny E. Morris and Charles M. Olsen, *Discerning God's Will Together: A Spiritual Practice for the Church* (Nashville: Upper Room, 1997), 35.

[7]Ibid., 58–59.

[8]Ibid.

[9]See "Designer Fruit," *http://www.fortune.com/fortune/smallbusiness/articles/0,15114,832334,00.html.* Designer fruit is all the rage. I recently ate a "grapple," an apple that tastes like a grape. Many fruits of this type are the handiwork of Floyd Zaiger, the most prolific fruit breeder in the world. Rather than attempt genetic modifications, Zaiger and others accelerate the natural selection process through hand-pollination.

¹⁰William Zinsser, *Writing about Your Life: A Journey into the Past* (New York: Marlowe and Company, 2004), 148.

¹¹Brian S. Mackay, *Freedom of the Christian* (New York and Nashville: Abingdon Press, 1965), 42.

¹²James M. Kouzes and Barry Z. Posner, *Credibility: How Leaders Gain and Lose It, Why People Demand It* (San Francisco: Jossey-Bass, 1993).

¹³Cited in Joseph L. Badaracco, Jr., *Defining Moments: When Managers Must Choose between Right and Right* (Boston: Harvard Business School, 1997), p. 9.

¹⁴Joseph Badaracco, in *Defining Moments*, 101, notes that the philosopher Nietzsche realized that self-definition is a lifelong process: "The creation of the self is not a static episode, a final goal which, once attained, forecloses the possibility of continuing to change and develop."

Chapter 6: Challenging 101

¹Edwin Friedman, who expanded Bowen family systems theory into leadership practice, used this expression to frame his final but unfinished manuscript, *A Failure of Nerve: Leadership in the Age of the Quick Fix.* This material is now available from the Edwin Friedman Estate, 6 Wynkoop Court, Bethesda, Maryland 20816. The introduction sets out Friedman's agenda clearly, "The emphasis here will be on strength, not pathology, on challenge, not comfort, on self-differentiation, not herding for togetherness. This is a difficult perspective to maintain in a 'seatbelt society' more oriented toward safety than adventure." Additionally, Guilford Publishers, 72 Spring Street, New York, N.Y., produced a video program, "Reinventing Leadership," with a study guide shortly before Friedman's death. It reflects the same ideas as the incomplete manuscript.

²Laurie Beth Jones, *Jesus, Life Coach: Learn from the Best* (Nashville: Thomas Nelson, 2004), 33.

³Max DePree, *Leadership Is an Art* (New York: Dell, 1989), 11.

⁴A research-based model for leaders is developed by James M. Kouzes and Barry Z. Posner in *The Leadership Challenge: How to Keep Getting Extraordinary Things Done in Organizations* (San Francisco: Jossey-Bass, 1995). This model identifies two mission-oriented leadership practices that link to the challenging process: challenging the process and inspiring a shared vision.

⁵Harper Lee, *To Kill a Mockingbird* (Philadelphia: Lippincott, 1960: reprint New York: HarperCollins, 2002), 128.

⁶Merom Klein and Rod Napier, *The Courage to Act: Five Factors of Courage to Transform Business* (Palo Alto, Calif.: Davies-Black, 2003), 40.

⁷John Keegan, *The Mask of Command* (New York: Viking Penguin, 1987), 13–91. The leading military historian in the world today, Keegan charts the process of generals' becoming less and less directly involved with troops on the firing line. Obviously, leaders who are personally at risk have a different view of the battle than those who are distant from it. With today's sophisticated spy satellites, commanders may not even be in the same country or on the same continent as their soldiers. Connecting, centering, and challenging are all more problematic for leaders when they try to lead by remote control.

⁸Warren Bennis, "What Is Courage?" *Fast Company* (September 2004): 101.

⁹George Barna, *The Power of Vision* (Ventura, Calif.: Regal Books, 1992), 28. Barna defines vision as "a clear mental image of a preferable future imparted by God to His chosen servants and is based upon a an accurate understanding of God, self and circumstance." He's correct that a focused picture or vision is basic and that the entire context is critical to effective leadership. Barna seems to elevate leaders so far above faith communities that vision is limited to and becomes the primary province of the leader.

¹⁰This definition of vision is mine, but the "outsight" term is from Kouzes and Posner, *The Leadership Challenge,* 45.

[11]Daniel H. Pink, "Revenge of the Right Brain," *Wired* (February 2005): 70–72. For an additional perspective on intuitive decision-making, see Malcolm Gladwell, *Blink: The Power of Thinking without Thinking* (New York: Little, Brown, 2005); and Danielle Sacks, "The Accidental Guru," *Fast Company* (January 2005): 64–69.

[12]Two classic explorations of creative thinking are Roger van Oech's *A Whack on the Side of the Head: How to Unlock Your Mind for Innovation* (New York: Warner Books, 1983) and *A Kick in the Seat of the Pants: Using Your Explorer, Artist, Judge, and Warrior to Be More Creative* (New York: Harper and Row, 1986).

[13]Betty Edwards, *Drawing on the Artist Within: A Guide to Innovation, Invention, Imagination, and Creativity* (New York: Simon and Schuster, 1986), 11–13.

[14]Ibid., 125–227. Edwards makes it plain that any artistic expression is basically the result of clear thinking and crisp seeing. Other treatments of artistic thinking and visioning include Michael J. Gelb, *How to Think Like Leonardo da Vinci: Seven Steps to Genius Every Day* (New York: Delacorte Press, 1998); Daniel J. Boorstin, *The Creators: A History of Heroes of the Imagination* (New York: Random House, 1992); and Michael Schrage, *Serious Play: How the World's Best Companies Simulate to Innovate* (Boston, Mass.: Harvard Business School Press, 2000).

[15]Mary Catherine Bateson, *Peripheral Vision* (New York: HarperCollins, 1994), 53.

[16]John Shelton Reed has produced a wide variety of studies on Southern culture, including *Southern Folk, Plain and Fancy* (Athens: University of Georgia Press, 1986), *One South: an Ethnic Approach to Regional Culture* (Baton Rouge: Louisiana State University Press, 1982), and "The South: What Is It? Where Is It?" in *The South for New Southerners,* ed. Paul D. Escott and David Goldfield (Chapel Hill: University of North Carolina Press, 1991).

[17]Edwin C. Nevis, Joan Lancourt, and Helen G. Vassallo, *Intentional Revolutions: A Seven-Point Strategy for Transforming Organizations* (San Francisco: Jossey-Bass, 1996), 67–248.

[18]Conrad Hyers, *And God Created Laughter: The Bible as Divine Comedy* (Atlanta: John Knox Press, 1987), 3.

[19]Ibid., 61.

[20]Anne Underwood, "We've Got Rhythm," *Newsweek* (October 11, 2004): 46.

Chapter 7: Cultivating Leadership Structures

[1]Walter Truett Anderson, *All Connected Now: Life in the First Global Civilization* (Boulder, Colo.: Westview Press, 2001), 160.

[2]Rosabeth Moss Kanter, *Evolve: Succeeding in the Digital Culture of Tomorrow* (Boston: Harvard Business School, 2001), 170.

[3]If you live in any of thirteen western states, you may choose to refer to the Sunset Zone maps. They are more precise growth guides than the USDA maps since they take into account the high temperatures, humidity levels, rainfall patterns, and the general length of growing seasons for different areas.

[4]Four-legged animals have spines that don't carry weight in the same way as humans' backs do. I was surprised that our family dog walked as soon as he woke up from his back surgery to repair a deteriorated disk. But his back was actually freed up, making him pain-free for the first time in a long time.

[5]I, and others, have provided life stage models on congregational health. My 1981 book, *To Dream Again,* has now been republished by the textbook specialists Wipf and Stock in Portland, Oregon, bringing its "provolutionary" model back into circulation.

[6]Peter Vaill, *Managing as a Performing Art* (San Francisco: Jossey-Bass, 1989), 2; Charles J. Palus, "Permanent White Water: Playing with the Metaphor," *Issues and Observations* 15, no. 1, (1995): 7–9; and Robert D. Dale, *Leadership for a Changing Church: Charting the Shape of the River* (Nashville: Abingdon Press, 1998), 119–20.

[7]Obviously, human tissue and organ transplants are more complicated to do successfully than grafts of plants. In spite of that obvious fact, some types of medical transplants have flourished for more than a century.

[8]Claire L. Gaudiani, "Wisdom as Capital in Prosperous Communities" in *The Community of the Future,* ed. Frances Hesselbein et al. (San Francisco: Jossey-Bass, 1998), 59–61.

[9]Dave Ulrich, "Six Practices for Creating Communities of Value, Not Proximity," in *The Community of the Future,* 157.

Chapter 8: Harvesting Leadership Strategy

[1]Henry Mintzberg, "Crafting Strategy," *Harvard Business Review* Reprint No. 87407 (Boston: Harvard Business School, 1987).

[2]Rosabeth Moss Kanter, *Evolve: Succeeding in the Digital Culture of Tomorrow* (Boston: Harvard Business School, 2001), 107.

[3]This is a model and process I developed in Robert D. Dale, *Leading Edge: Leadership Strategies from the New Testament* (Nashville: Abingdon Press, 1996).

[4]Martin Luther, quoted and translated in Roland H. Bainton, *Here I Stand: A Life of Martin Luther* (New York and Nashville: Abingdon Press, 1950), 185.

[5]There's an additional element of strategy in the New Testament. The Book of Revelation suggests what leaders can do when their worlds fall in on them. They can do what's feasible to survive so they can return to the "focus with flexibility on the future" cycle again. See Dale, *Leading Edge,* 105–15.

[6]Bruce Wilkinson, *The Prayer of Jabez: Breaking through to the Blessed Life* (Sisters, Oreg.: Multnomah, 2000), iii.

[7]For a discussion of Lewis's "good infection," see Robert Sokolowski's *Eucharistic Presence: A Study in the Theology of Disclosure* (Washington, D.C.: Catholic University of America Press, 1994), 36.

[8]Aaron Lynch, *Thought Contagion: How Belief Spreads through Society* (New York: Basic Books, 1996), 1–39.

[9]Ibid., 107–14.

[10]Malcolm Gladwell, *The Tipping Point: How Little Things Make a Big Difference* (Boston: Little, Brown, 2000).

[11]Albert-Laszlo Barabasi, *Linked: The New Science of Networks* (Cambridge, Mass.: Perseus Publishing, 2002), 161–78.

[12]Anthony T. Jones and Adam Westwood, "Power from the Oceans," *The Futurist* (January-February, 2005): 37–41.

Chapter 9: Planting Leadership Processes

[1]Jean Lipman-Blumen, *Connective Leadership: Managing in a Changing World* (New York: Oxford University Press, 1996), 46–76. For a classic perspective on the impact of the frontier experience on the American psyche, see Frederick Jackson Turner, *The Frontier in American History* (New York: Henry Holt and Company, 1920).

[2]Appreciative inquiry—exploration that increases the value of the community— builds on a few central assumptions. I've adapted this list from Mark Lau Branson's *Memories, Hopes, and Conversations* (Herndon, Va.: Alban Institute, 2004), 24.

[3]For an interesting treatment of time and futurity, see Asa Briggs and Daniel Snowman, eds., *Fins de Siecle: How Centuries End 1400–2000* (New Haven, Conn.: Yale University Press, 1996).

[4]A variety of resources lend a process perspective to leaders. From a systems' viewpoint, Mary Beth O'Neill's *Executive Coaching with Backbone and Heart: A Systems Approach to Engaging Leaders with Their Challenges* (San Francisco: Jossey-Bass, 2000) and Israel Galindo's *The Hidden Lives of Congregations: Discerning Church Dynamics* (Herndon, Va.: Alban Institute, 2004) rely on Bowen theory as an anchor. O'Neill's

title itself reflects Bowen theory, with "backbone" referring to taking stands, and "heart" calling on leaders to stay connected to their communities. The Bowen view of human interaction is the foundation for this book. From a leaders' communication angle, Jane Magruder Watkins and Bernard J. Mohr's *Appreciative Inquiry: Change at the Speed of Imagination* (San Francisco: Jossey-Bass/Pfieffer, 2001); Mark Lau Branson's *Memories, Hopes, and Conversations* (Herndon, Va.: Alban Institute, 2004); Gail T. Fairhurst and Robert A. Sarr's *The Art of Framing: Managing the Language of Leadership* (San Francisco: Jossey-Bass, 1996); Annette Simmons's *A Safe Place for Dangerous Truths: Using Dialogue to Overcome Fear and Distrust at Work* (New York: AMACOM, 1999); Linda Ellinor and Glenna Gerard's *Dialogue: Rediscover the Transforming Power of Conversation* (New York: John Wiley, 1998); Stanley L. Payne's *The Art of Asking Questions* (Princeton, N.J.: Princeton University Press, 1951); and William Ury's *Getting to Peace: Transforming Conflict at Home, at Work, and in the World* (New York: Viking Press, 1999) provide a rich array of effective ways leaders can listen, learn, speak, and relate. From a facilitation perspective, Dale Hunter, Anne Bailey, and Bill Taylor's *The Art of Facilitation: How to Create Group Synergy* (Tucson, Ariz.: Fisher Books, 1995) and Richard C. Weaver and John D. Farrell's *Managers as Facilitators: A Practical Guide to Getting Work Done in a Changing Workplace* (San Francisco: Berrett-Koehler, 1997) show ways to help decisions flow.

[5]David D. Chrislip and Carl E. Larson, *Collaborative Leadership: How Citizens and Civic Leaders Make a Difference* (San Francisco: Jossey-Bass, 1994), 79.

[6]Ibid., 160–63.

[7]John Kotter, *A Force for Change: How Leadership Differs from Management* (New York: Free Press, 1990), 83.

[8]Peter Drucker, cited in Bob Buford's *Finishing Well: What People Who Really Live Do Differently* (Nashville: Integrity Publishers, 2004), 8.

[9]Ronald W. Richardson, *Becoming a Healthier Pastor: Family Systems Theory and the Pastor's Own Family* (Minneapolis: Fortress Press, 2005), 115–16.

[10]Fairhurst and Sarr, *The Art of Framing*.

[11]Watkins and Mohr, *Appreciative Inquiry*, 134.

[12]See "Chronic Anxiety" in Michael E. Kerr and Murray Bowen, *Family Evaluation: An Approach Based on Bowen Theory* (New York: W. W. Norton, 1988), 112–33.